BLISSFUL IGNORANCE

LIVE a BLIG LIFE!

Simplicity is the future
complexity!

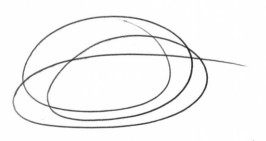

BLISSFUL IGNORANCE

THE ART OF BEING AN ENTREPRENEUR

CASSIDY PHILLIPS

FOUNDER OF TRIGGERPOINT

LIONCREST
PUBLISHING

BLISSFUL IGNORANCE
The Art of Being an Entrepreneur

ISBN   978-1-5445-1317-1 *Paperback*
       978-1-5445-1316-4 *Ebook*

Dear Heavenly Father, I am a man in thanks for all You've given me here on earth. I was broken, beat down, and confused, yet rebuilt with Your guidance and clarity. Please allow me to be a funnel for every word You give me. Allow this book to communicate to all those who are in need of a greater quality of life as an entrepreneur. I am thankful for my wonderful wife and my two amazing children for staying by my side as I pursue my purpose-driven path.

In Jesus's name, amen.

CONTENTS

FOREWORD

2001

- This was one of the hardest years of my life. I watched my body become a lean and powerful swimming, biking, and running machine. However, at the same time, my insides broke down, and every movement became difficult for me. Life would never be the same.
- I studied muscle tissue fiber structure and how to regenerate it. I married that with my biomechanical background and created a line of products that would allow me to work on myself just as a therapist would. I spent the remainder of my time studying the Bible to get a better understanding of who Jesus was. I had

no interest in religion, but I loved the Jesus dude the Bible talked about. I redefined my thought processes and learned to rely on myself.

- Without knowing it, I started building the foundations for TriggerPoint education and products.
- I met the woman of my dreams.
- I had an internal fear that I had multiple sclerosis. Doctors diagnosed my body breakdown as fibromyalgia.

2002

- After months of self-discipline, I noticed a significant change in the way my body moved and felt. I returned to all the doctors who said I had a sixty-year-old's back and that I'd never be an athlete again. They were shocked by the changes and, quite frankly, unwilling to even recognize them.
- I wanted to share this newfound confidence and knowledge of my body with others. I decided to turn my products, which I'd originally created for myself, into a company. On the same day I launched the company, I also asked my fantastic girlfriend, Carin Garvin, to marry me. I proposed to Carin and launched my company at the Gulf Coast Triathlon. All I had was a single product at the time (which you'll learn about later), but that was all I needed. People were shocked at how well my product worked. I pro-

posed to Carin at the end of the race when she was tired—she had to say yes!

- November was the first tipping point. Carin and I had a booth at the Florida IRONMAN. Looking back, it was pathetic, but the booth did its job. We had all of our products packaged and ready to sell.

- We actually went to the local Walmart, bought foam blocks for five dollars, and bundled them with my products to resell for ten dollars. By the end of the event, we had sold everything—grossing more than $5,000 in sales. And the people who didn't buy anything walked away from our booth educated about how they could take better care of their bodies. This was when I first realized we had something special! It wasn't about the product we sold. It was about how our product could change people's lives.

- I found an amazing family in Atlanta to help with the cutting and sewing of our products. They started producing about fifty products for us per week, but as our orders increased, we eventually outgrew them. (These products included TP Balls, Foot Ballers, and Quadballers.)

2003

- I bought a 1973 Airstream, a Ford truck, hired an employee, and hit the road to sell our products. By this time, Carin and I had been married for five months, but she stayed in Atlanta as my employee, and I hit the road.

- Our first event was unbelievable. I called a mentor of mine and told him, "This must be how Jesus felt: we have people coming to our booth in walkers, using our products, and leaving the booth without them, all singing our praises." We sold out of everything yet again.

- Carin took care of everything I couldn't: supply chain, bills, inventory—basically, all the important stuff. She'd fly to and from each event, work all weekend, then return to her corporate day job and do our books and supply chain at night. This was great for the company but very difficult for her.

- By the end of 2003, things were crazy. We had twenty suppliers, and we were making hundreds of thousands in sales.

- Our supply chain started to crumble, and attending events every weekend started to take a toll on my wife and our marriage.

- We were actually making parts of our products on the road, shipping them to Atlanta (where the products were assembled, cut, and sewn), then sent back to us on the road for each event. This was not a sustainable model.

- By midyear, Carin had had enough of staying at home. It was time for her to hit the road. At one point, we had two employees, one dog, and Carin and myself traveling in the Ford truck and the Airstream. We would ship products from each city we drove through.

2004

- We had driven through just about every state by this point, so we decided to upgrade our operation. Upgrading, for us, meant selling the Airstream and truck to buy a motor home. That still wasn't enough. Carin and I had been married for a while, and my wife needed a home. The business was thriving, and Jon, our one true employee, was tired of being on the road. It was time to get an office, find a home, and build this company.
- We landed in Austin, Texas. Carin and I rented a little house with an office in it. Once we had a chance to look at the numbers, we realized that we'd done more than a million dollars in sales on the road, and we nearly crapped our pants.
- We doubled down on the education side of our business. Our next hire was for graphic design and marketing. We continued to go from event to event, and we were getting calls every day from retailers that wanted to carry our products.

2005

- To this point, we had grown all of this from a $17,000

loan from my grandmother, but now we needed more cash to take our production overseas. We paid Grandmother Mimi back the money we owed her. Carin and I were living off $100 a week after personal expenses.

- We got endorsements from the six athletes who went to the 2004 Summer Olympics for triathlon.
- With those relationships established, we were poised to grow.

2006

- We'd done more than $5 million in sales; we had a few employees in operations, marketing, and sales; and we had so many inbound sales calls that it blew my mind.
- We could not keep up with production demand in the United States.
- My wife was done—done with HR, done with helping supply chain, and done with working with the company altogether...and she was pregnant.
- We'd tapped out the triathlon market, so now it was time to push hard into retail sales. Then I put a target on the fitness industry.
- Continuing education would play a big role in getting our products into trainers' hands. The more they used our products, the more people bought them.

2007

- By this time, we had a handful of employees, a real office, and a warehouse, and we were doing millions a year in sales. Yet we were still struggling to make a profit.

- We needed money for overseas production, so I called three triathletes who had benefitted greatly from the use of the products and the education I had created. The triathletes invested in TriggerPoint to take our production overseas—boy did they end up getting a huge win!

- A few dollars later, and with roughly 10 percent of my company sold, we took production overseas.

- In April, a few weeks after my son Sklar was born, I left for China. I was there for three weeks—just long enough to set up production.

- This was the hardest three weeks of my life up until that point. Nothing went right. I didn't speak the language, I didn't know the social norms, and I didn't like the food. I was hours outside of Shanghai, yet I knew I was on the right path.

2008

- The economy took a turn for the worse. We had premium products, and products deliver premium results, but we didn't know if the industry would be willing to pay high prices for our products as the overall market made a correction.

- I created a product called the Grid around this time. The Grid was a perfectly crafted foam roller. No one had anything like it. Most people rolled their muscles on a swim noodle if they weren't using our products.
- We defined the industry with our revolutionary products and defined price points that defined the foam-rolling industry.
- Along with the new products came the birth of our second son, Pace. The kids were seventeen months apart, and my wife became a full-time mom.

2009

- This year was a blur.

2010

- TriggerPoint had become a household brand, and the Grid was the hero product of the company. Container after container shipped around the world. Production was very difficult to manage.
- We leveraged our popularity into partnerships with IMG Academy, Athletes Performance, and other major organizations.
- Our products started being used in movies and TV shows for product placement.
- We went to the NFL combine and created a dedicated push into organized sports.

2011

- We got to forty employees, had a gym, and had distributors around the world.
- International flights became a normal pattern in my everyday life.
- My body started to get tired. We were selling massive quantities of products, but our manufacturing demands became heartburn for me.
- We'd increased our sales to more than $10 million a year.
- We expanded our digital footprint on the web and added products to the Grid line.
- I struggled personally and professionally to maintain a positive outlook on my ability to manage our growth, both externally with manufacturing and distribution and internally with employees.

2012

- The London Olympics this year was the greatest tipping point in our company's history.
- Before the Olympics, we delivered our products to Team USA's training facilities in Spain. We also sent products to their Olympic village in London. Shortly thereafter, images of LeBron James, Kobe Bryant, and others using our products circulated in the media.
- The Grid was now on every sideline in the NFL and the NBA.

- Mark Wahlberg was photographed carrying one of our products into a training session.
- David Beckham was photographed getting onto his plane with a Grid.
- We had just under fifty employees.
- Our educational classes were being taught globally, and we had distribution in more than fifty countries.

2013

- Sales increased to more than $15 million.
- Our staff grew so large that HR became hard to manage.
- Our manufacturing and supply chain was difficult to keep up with.
- We were in thousands of retailers around the world.
- I increased the number of products we sold, along with our education and marketing efforts.
- I was exhausted and needed a break.
- This was the hardest year of my life. I made some poor decisions, recovered from those decisions, and continued to grow.
- By the end of 2013, I made a goal to sell the company within twelve months.

2014

- Sales increased to just under $20 million.

- Our marketing efforts were now more focused on our products rather than our education.
- I sold TriggerPoint on October 17.

bliss·ful
ˈblisfəl/
Adjective

1. Extremely happy; full of joy.

"A blissful couple holding a baby."

2. Providing perfect happiness or great joy.

"The blissful caress of cool cotton sheets."

Synonyms: happy, euphoric, joyful, elated, rapturous, delighted, thrilled, overjoyed, joyous, on cloud nine, in seventh heaven, over the moon, on top of the world.

ig·no·rance
ˈignərəns/
Noun

1. Lack of knowledge or information.

"He acted in ignorance of basic procedures."

Synonyms: lack of knowledge, lack of education, foolishness, incomprehension of, unawareness of.

Combined, these two words create blissful ignorance: the joy of not knowing how easy or how difficult a situation may be—as though you are looking at life through the lens of a child.

INTRODUCTION

I launched my company, TriggerPoint, at the exact moment when everything in my life had broken down around me.

My professors in college told me that I'd never perform at a university level. After I dropped out of college, my dad cut me off financially. I moved to LA, and I was successful as an actor, but I never felt fulfilled. I had two companies go bust while living in California. My aggressive nature busted up several relationships. Just when I thought I found the right woman and moved to Atlanta, the relationship sizzled out.

Then, as if that wasn't enough, my body started to break down, and no doctor could tell me what was going on. This was horrible, as my body and what I could accomplish with it—my triathlons, adventure racing, stunts, skating, cycling, jumping out of airplanes—was my *identity*.

Holy crap—I'd gone from longtime hero, in my own eyes, to zero overnight.

I didn't know who I was supposed to be—not when I was a kid, not in LA, not in Atlanta. I got so used to living within the confines of my own insecurities that I finally stopped having faith in myself.

The message I got from every area of my life was the same: I didn't fit in, and I had nothing to offer the world.

If only I knew how wrong I was.

THIS IS A LOVE STORY ABOUT BUSINESS—AND FAITH

This book is a feel-good tale about watching your life go to ruins and having everything important to you get taken away. It's a how-to manual for losing your confidence and tapping into your deepest insecurities.

Most of all, this is a story about how much you can do when you don't know what you're doing.

This is the story of how to become an entrepreneur.

There are plenty of entrepreneurs who suffer from paralysis by analysis. They're afraid of trying something new. They're worried about what others will think and say. Beyond the fear of not accomplishing what you set out to achieve, there's also the insecurity of walking with faith that you are making the right choices.

But in the blink of an eye, everything can change. When I lost faith in everything, I found a new relationship with Jesus—not the church or the religion but the man who gave everything for me to be me. In a very short time, this newfound relationship gave me the confidence to believe in myself.

With this newfound confidence, I launched a fitness equipment company that I felt was going to change the world. I was now seeing through clear eyes, was able to learn from my past, and was able to apply those lessons to my future.

Before long, I found my wonderful wife, became comfortable in my own skin, and built an amazing company. My struggles became my motivator, not my roadblock. I realized that my purpose was not to prove something to someone but rather to provide a product and education to people looking to improve their quality of life.

I threw out all reasoning, bought an Airstream trailer and

a truck, and set out with my wife, an employee, and a dog to change the world. We lived on the road, preaching the word of TriggerPoint, receiving and shipping orders as we went.

As I got feedback from those around me that the products and education were changing the way that they moved— not only physically but mentally as well—I had to go all in. I felt like Christ walking with those who were in need of his message.

The foundation for every move we made was based in the word of Christ, not religion. Our mission was simple: educate the people we were selling to and allow them to make their own purchasing decision.

Our mission wasn't about making money; it was about helping people in need.

Some might say our formula was all wrong for a newly married couple, but it was just right for us. We preferred to swim upstream and change the world rather than swim downstream and be safe with all the others.

At the time, we had no idea if this was going to work, but we had faith—faith in who we were and what we were doing and faith in the Lord. Not a bad way to start!

PASSION, COMMITMENT, AND HARD WORK

These days, there's a lot of cachet around being an entrepreneur. When I started in business for myself, though, most people put entrepreneurs right up there with crackpot inventors and evangelical missionaries.

Worst-case scenario, they thought you were crazy. Best-case scenario, they'd wish you luck and walk away shaking their heads.

Today, people look at entrepreneurship as just another career choice. The digital revolution has transformed entrepreneurship from an oddity to a commodity. Far from being a fringe movement, people consider being an entrepreneur a glamorous career decision.

As a result, the air is buzzing with catchphrases such as "Follow your passion" and "Screw the nine to five." There are even university courses in entrepreneurship now, not to mention hundreds of self-appointed gurus who claim that starting your own business is as easy as paying $99.99 for their online course.

Don't buy the hype. If you're lucky, those products only waste your money. If you're less lucky, it will waste years of your life—years where you sink all your focus and energy into a business scheme that never brings you real fulfillment. In the process, you'll lose friendships, marriages, and relationships with your children, all because you lacked the essential core traits that make entrepreneurship possible.

Don't make that mistake. Being an entrepreneur requires *passion*, *commitment*, and a *dedication to excellence*, every single day. It's risky, but in the end, if following your passion is paired with hard work and faith, you'll be successful.

FINDING YOUR BLISS...IN IGNORANCE

More often than you realize, what you view as a weakness is a strength in other people's eyes.

I have ADD, ADHD, and dyslexia, so I inevitably think differently from most people. This, of course, can cause friction with others because they are "textbook" thinkers who never venture out of the "box" they were taught in school. I always saw the standards as safe and anything outside of the box as exciting.

That's what makes me such a great entrepreneur. And if you're reading this book, you almost certainly have the same inclination to redefine what constitutes "normal." Your success and your bliss won't come to you the same way it does for everyone else.

Success is a relative term anyway: one person's success

is another person's failure. People might look at all of my so-called learning disabilities and see them as an obstacle to success. But to me, they make me who I am today, and I'm happy about that. What other people view as ignorance is a big part of my bliss.

Ignorance will always lead you back to the customer, the person you exist to serve. Ignorance will nourish the emotional connection that makes the entrepreneurial life richer than one focused on wealth. Ignorance will expand the boundaries of your creativity by freeing you from fear.

You must find your bliss in ignorance. Otherwise, you might as well stay in a safe corporate job. My goal with this book is to help you zero in on your own bliss through the ignorance and successes of my own entrepreneurial story.

THIS ISN'T PAINT BY NUMBERS—IT'S AN ART

It takes a certain kind of person to be an entrepreneur. It takes someone who gets a kick out of living on the edge. Someone who enjoys proving to everyone that they don't have to do things the way society has set out for them. Someone who gets more joy out of blazing their own trail than taking the five-lane interstate, even if it means a lot more bumps and bruises.

Above all, it takes someone who enjoys work for work's sake. You have to freaking hustle.

Still, the leading perceptions of being an entrepreneur cause some of the most passionate people to overthink their process. If you're one of those people who feels compelled to prove their success with material possessions—fancy cars and houses you can't afford—you're not cut out for this.

At the end of the day, the kind of entrepreneur—and person—you are has nothing to do with the kind of car you drive.

The business-building "gurus" want you to believe that they can help you by selling you books, courses, memberships, and workshops. They want to foster the belief that adding just one more tool to your process means your business will be a slam-dunk success from day one.

But it doesn't work like that. Entrepreneurship is an art, not a science. For someone to give you a set of steps to business success is like giving you a paint-by-numbers coloring book and promising your work will end up on the wall of the Louvre.

History's greatest works of art were those that created new definitions of what art could be. In the same way, the greatest companies are those that created a market where a market didn't exist before. The best part about this type of mindset is that it allows you to make all your own rules, like a successful entrepreneur should.

To do this, you must start from a place of no definitions. You must be willing to act like you know nothing. You must be willing to be ignorant yet passionate about learning whatever it is that you don't know, all for the greater good of your customers.

That's exactly where I started, and it's exactly where you can start too.

A HUMAN APPROACH

The freedom you crave as an entrepreneur is ultimately not defined by your lifestyle, your schedule, your finances, or even your creativity. It's about being unfettered, in your heart and mind, to do *whatever it takes* to achieve your goals.

Corporate jobs make it easy to think we can compartmentalize our work and isolate it from the rest of our lives. Starting your own business doesn't allow you that luxury. As an entrepreneur, you *are* your business. The success of the company you're trying to build is intrinsically linked to your success as a human being.

So in order to succeed, I will detail a few ways you're going to have to redefine your thought process in this book:

1. NOBODY WILL BE IMPRESSED BY THE SACRIFICES YOU MAKE

Defining your own path requires tremendous sacrifice. You can't make those sacrifices with the expectation that anyone else will notice or pat you on the back.

2. NOTHING IS AS COMPLEX AS THE "EXPERTS" MAKE IT OUT TO BE

Your business might be complex, but your purpose is simple: to serve a need that other people have. Without that need, you don't have a business. As a human, you exist for one purpose: to serve other people through relationships. Without those relationships, you won't have a fulfilling life, no matter how much material "success" you achieve.

3. TOO MUCH PROCESS WILL KILL THE PASSION

This book exists to help you stop being hung up on process. Despite what anyone may tell you, business is not a paint-by-numbers formula. It's a living, dynamic organism that reacts unpredictably and often defies explanation.

THE GOOD NEWS: YOU AREN'T SPECIAL

This book will not help you create a new version of someone else's success. It won't guide you to hitting your first million dollars, your first million customers, or any other arbitrarily chosen success marker.

Instead, it will give you practical guidance in finding the purpose-driven path of your business. It's the difference between a dating app that helps you find a one-night stand and a matchmaker who helps you find the person you want to marry.

The fact that you aren't special is good news. It means that nothing that happens to you is an anomaly. Every trial you have faced and are about to face is one that every other entrepreneur has confronted in their own journey, including me. That is why I'm sharing it all—my successes and my failures—in this book: to help you endure on this amazing, painful, and difficult journey as an entrepreneur.

My career hasn't only been defined by creating a company that employed hundreds or making a product that helped millions. It's been in service of learning the hard lessons that I can pass on to dreamers just like you.

I can't tell you how to achieve the success you're dreaming of. I can only put the tools in your hands and remind you of one of the most basic and important lessons we often forget as outside-the-box dreamers:

> When your life gets so difficult—so draining and discouraging that you wonder how you'll even make it through the day—it's not the cars or the fancy homes that will push you through the struggles of the entrepreneurial life. The only thing that can drive you forward is the faith that the work itself will be its own reward.

CASSIDYISMS EXPLAINED

There are a lot of things I'd do differently now if I could do them all over again. I'd use the knowledge I gained in the hard yards of my preentrepreneurial life to find and follow the purpose-driven path of my business.

Fortunately, the lessons I learned while building TriggerPoint now have an irrevocable trigger for me thanks to something called Cassidyisms.

This term was coined by my employees, who heard me say the same set of short, memorable sayings over and over again. I'd formulated these sayings as my business grew, using them to apply to all areas of business and personal life.

A different Cassidyism will kick off almost every chapter—whether as a chapter title or as a quote—and provide you with the same shot of inspiration they offered my team.

CHAPTER 1

WHO AND WHAT I AM

If we're not growing, we're dying.

We spend most of our lives talking and very little of our lives listening. This tendency is germane to the entrepreneurial mindset. Combine a passionate personality, a brain given to hyperfocus, and a full slate of personal insecurities, and you've got a person ready to talk until you either buy what they're selling or drop from exhaustion.

For the longest time, I thought my hard work and my resulting achievements were what made me important. It took losing everything to realize that nobody cared how great a story I had.

All my talk was just me trying to sell the myth of my own value.

But the story of how I got to where I am today is the story of how I did everything wrong. Only when I embraced that story—the hubris, the vulnerabilities, and above all, the ignorance it reveals—was I able to discover my calling. Only through humility was I able to become the person I wanted to be.

THE GIFT OF EDUCATIONAL FAILURE

Like so many children of broken marriages, my parents' divorce left me with emotional wounds that went untreated. Their quick remarriages brought a slew of stepbrothers and stepsisters, followed quickly by half siblings, and left me wondering where I belonged in the family.

Because I never knew where to turn when I needed help, I decided I didn't need help. Instead, I cast myself as the careless but lovable scamp who clowned around in class but could charm the teachers into looking the other way.

Of course, my antics became less charming the more I failed in school. As a result, teachers thought I was either stubborn or stupid, so I shifted from class clown to con artist. In high school, I even found a teacher who was willing to give me the answers to the tests for the rest of the year. I bribed him with two frozen geese and some CDs (it was Louisiana. What did you expect?).

> The teachers might have seen me as ignorant—and it hurt at the time—but I'm grateful for what it taught me about business: I had to think outside the box and use my charm to move forward in life.

By the time I turned eighteen, I was ready to get the hell out of small-town Louisiana. I packed my car and drove to Colorado, where I planned to enter the world of professional cycling. Athletics had always been the one part of my life where I could be sure of getting the attention I desired, especially from my dad.

At age eight, I was already competing in BMX events. By age ten, I was medaling in triathlons. Throughout my school years, teachers always encouraged me in athletics over academics, suggesting that it was the one path where I had a real chance to excel. I resented their perception of me, but I also loved it. Sports were my escape from being the problem kid—the one place where I could prove my worth.

When I left Louisiana, I went to Metro State University in Denver for a year, got my grades up, and then transferred to the University of Colorado. I lasted only a semester at the University of Colorado, as I had a mental breakdown.

I was studying for hours upon hours, color-coding everything and posting it all on my wall in a desperate effort to learn.

But my grades were still horrible. Scantron tests had become the norm, all the bubbles blended together, reinforcing my inability to function within the strict guidelines of a university education. When I'd argue with my teachers that I knew the materials I was studying, they recommend that I go to the learning center.

It was there that it was finally explained to me that I had something called dyslexia. Unfortunately, this was their rationale for telling me that I'd never be able to perform at a university level.

Are you effing kidding me? I thought. *I've always been able to "perform." They had the audacity to tell me that I'd never be able to perform at a university level and that I needed to find a vocational school. Really? Are you kidding me? I'm giving it my best, and this is what I get in return? Eff you. I'm out.*

The structure of institutional learning got the win. I couldn't do it, so I had to get myself out of the university rat race "box." With a huge chip on my shoulder and the question "What the heck am I going to do with my life?" looming over me, I drove from the Rockies back down to the bayou in defeat.

I played it over and over in my head: *You're not good enough. You're slow. You're not smart.* One professor had even said to me, "I overcame dyslexia; so can you." I was full of rage at the institution for saying my academic struggles were the result of learning disabilities: severe dyslexia, audiovisual memory problems, and impaired perception of numbers and letters, on and on.

As I drove away from the University of Colorado, I imagined my tutors, my second grade teacher, and all these people who tried to help me along the way, all giving me a look that said, "This is going to be tough, but you're special. You learn differently. You're not like all the other kids."

Finally, it popped into my head: *I am special, and I will succeed on my own terms. I'll prove it to all of you. I'll go to Hollywood and be an actor!*

When I got back to Louisiana, I told my father my dream of becoming an actor.

"Well," he said, "you'd better get all you can get while you can get it. Because you're not going to get a dime from me once you leave Louisiana this time."

Those harsh words were the greatest gift he could have given me.

The chip on my shoulder that formed that day would power me through the coming years of struggle. That night, just after I'd returned home in defeat, I began a habit that I've continued ever since: I stood in front of the mirror, looked myself dead in the eye, and said, "You're *going* to do this."

I left Louisiana for a second time a week later. I had $500 in my pocket, and I was headed for the city that turns people into stars.

THE HOLLYWOOD HOPEFUL

Let's begin with the obvious: Los Angeles is no cure for insecurity. The entertainment industry reduces you to a numerical quantity. Everyone you meet in LA is gauging how much potential you have to make them money.

Realizing this brought all my self-doubt and insecurities to the surface. I had only traded one place where I felt inadequate—college—for another—the City of Angels. The only thing that saved me from running back home again was that chip on my shoulder. I was determined not to admit defeat. The cutthroat nature of show business played right into my determination. I knew that if I didn't want to end up on the street, I had to make it one way or another.

For all its flaws, the entertainment business has one great virtue: it's one of the last industries where you can be entirely self-made. If you know how to hustle, you have as much of a shot as anyone else does at succeeding.

Almost immediately, I hit my stride in commercials and stunt work. A combination of short scripts (which meant fewer words to memorize) and lots of available work made commercials the ideal place for me to start my career in the entertainment industry.

However, I wasn't content to be the lowest guy on the totem pole. My insecurities demanded that I distinguish myself from the bartenders, lifeguards, and the guys selling cigarettes at 7-Eleven, all of whom were actors auditioning for the same parts as me.

To get ahead of my competition, I started taking acting classes. In the process, I made friends with a few other guys who, like me, were looking for ways to rise above the herd of Hollywood hopefuls. We were hungry, we were ambitious, and we knew just enough to be dangerous.

Our shared hunger for success—and our blissful ignorance—allowed me to talk them all into putting together a play. In my view, it was the perfect way for us to exercise our talents and get in front of more people. My new actor friends all immediately objected.

What did we know about producing a play? Who would even come to see us?

We solved that problem by getting a gig at a local bar: the people we invited were sure to come if they knew they could drink! We were right: our show, *Spoon River*, ended up doing a sold-out run. People loved it, told their friends, and each night, we performed to a packed house. We went from acting class zeros to local heroes.

In the afterglow of that success, I hatched a new idea. This one was even crazier than the last. On the final night of our play, as we sat around drunkenly toasting our thespian genius, I uttered two sentences that changed the trajectory of my life forever:

"I want to make a movie. Who's in?"

THE NEW KID WITH THE GOLDEN TOUCH

Take a group of struggling no-name actors with minimal movie experience and no clue about production, throw in some donated film and editing software we learned on the fly, and subtract any hint of a budget.

What do you get? In the mid nineties, when we were doing all of this, you got the brand-new genre of movies called indie films.

A year after I announced my crazy idea, my friends and I were showing our movie at the Palm Springs Film Festival. For us, this was a major coup. We knew where festival acclaim could lead. Just down the hall from where our movie was screened, a group of guys just like us sold a shoestring film called *Swingers* to Miramax for $5 million.

We didn't sell our movie for that kind of money, but we did end up taking it around the world for a summer's worth of international film festivals. Our movie's success was timed perfectly with the breaking wave of independent media. I'd proven that I could do something right, and Hollywood assumed it meant I could do it again.

In Los Angeles, being in the right place at the right time means one thing: deals.

I won't lie—this success was a little bit of a power buzz. Once I felt that buzz and the recognition that came with it, I wanted more.

More came in the form of creating my own production company with three other industry pros. Right off the bat, we raised some serious money. We set ourselves up in an office on Rodeo Drive. When I wasn't taking meetings, working on set, or having fun as a stuntman, I peacocked around town in a Zanetti suit, hair combed back, cigarette hanging from my mouth like James Dean. I celebrated my twenty-seventh birthday on the Sunset Strip with 350 guests.

I felt like a king, and for a brief moment of time, my insecurities vanished.

As a result of my superficial success, I'd become the most selfish person my friends knew, and in Los Angeles, that's saying something.

I soon learned the lesson that every show business rookie must learn at some point: everyone in LA is a buddy, but you have no real friends in that city. You can spend years proving yourself, but as soon as you stop making people money, you're right back to square one.

For me, that tipping point came courtesy of a script I represented. It was a great screwball comedy with a hilarious concept, all based on a real-life situation. It was easy to see Adam Sandler or Chris Rock starring in it. My production company shopped it around in full confidence of selling it to one of the big studios.

However, after months of meetings, I still had no buyers for the script, and my partners lost confidence in my golden touch. One day, I got a warning call from one of them.

"We're kicking you out of the company tomorrow," he

said. "If there's anything you want, you should get it now while you still can."

It wasn't lost on me that this was exactly what my dad said to me when I left Louisiana. As quickly as my dreams had caught fire, they had burned out. Once again, I was left with nothing but myself.

FROM BLISSFUL TO BROKEN

Then I met a girl.

It was the kind of coincidence you'd never believe if you saw it in a movie. I was at a birthday party for a friend when a girl walked out of the crowd. In LA, good-looking women are a dime a dozen. You stop even noticing them after a while.

She was from the South, same as me. Stranger still, she knew who I was. Her cousin had been a friend of mine in high school, and I'd helped her cousin through some hard times. In fact, this girl had read all about me in her cousin's diary. In this girl's mind, I was a strong, sensitive, real-life hero.

Long story short, I moved east with her. I got into real estate and picked up training again, this with the intention of being a competitive triathlete. Despite my newfound purpose in life, living in a new place and being in a new relationship brought up all my insecurities yet again. The only way I knew to deal with those insecurities was to rely on physical accomplishments.

I didn't know how to talk to people unless I was talking about the amazing things I'd done that week—a marathon I was training for, the miles I biked, or the hours I'd spent swimming that morning.

But something had shifted in the transition between California and the Deep South: training in the sweltering heat was taking a serious toll on my body, and I wasn't recovering the way I used to.

Then suddenly, I discovered that this girl, the one I'd moved to Atlanta with, was cheating on me.

Everything that had once helped me compensate for my insecurities—my girlfriend, my show business success, my physical achievements—was disappearing from my life. The only thing I could think to do was keep training. If I could just get my health back, enough to finish each week's athletic event, I felt like I could keep moving forward with my life.

I did IVs of Vitamin C, glutathione and B12 injections, and over three hundred shots of procaine. I visited every

specialist in town, from Western MDs to holistic practitioners. But they all told me different versions of the
same thing: I had beaten my body into nothing. I had
the muscle wear of a sixty-year-old. One of them finally
leveled with me.

"Look, your body isn't responding to any of the treat-
ments. You may want to get checked for the possibility
of multiple sclerosis."

Hearing him say that was like a death sentence. Throughout
this physical breakdown, I'd always assumed that at some
point, some doctor would figure out what was wrong and
take care of it, and I'd be back to normal. It never occurred
to me that I might be beyond the point of being cured.

I'd always thought of myself as self-reliant. It suddenly
dawned on me that everything I did, from making a film
with my friends to jumping out of planes to moving to
Atlanta, made me feel entitled to other people's love and
care. This was why I could only ever talk about myself. My
entire life was a giant desperate act of begging people to
care for me.

I went home from the clinic that day, looked at myself in
the mirror, and said to my face what I was finally seeing.

"You keep looking for someone—anyone—to take care of

you. You've seen every specialist in town. You've tried every solution imaginable. And none of it has worked. It's time for you to take care of yourself."

> You can find outside help to solve your problems, but at the end of the day, you're an entrepreneur for a reason: you think outside the box and want to help people. Sometimes you have to do that yourself.

BECOMING A STUDENT

Having been an athlete all my life, I thought I understood all about how the body moved. In reality, my good health had allowed me to remain blissfully ignorant of the muscular structure that made those movements possible.

Taking on the duty of healing myself meant leaning into that ignorance and finding out how much I didn't know. I stayed up all night researching articles on the internet, educating myself on muscle tissue, its fiber and structure, how it functioned, how it responded to injury, and how it regenerated.

Through my research, I learned that the body breaks down into a series of fulcrums and levers. Ultimate strength and flexibility are simply a matter of accessing those fulcrums and levers and using them repeatedly to build efficiency of movement.

For once, I didn't need anyone to recognize or praise me for my education. The knowledge was its own reward. And by applying that knowledge, I was healing my body in real time.

There was another big difference, too, one that would have shocked anyone who knew me in the past.

My ex, the one I'd moved to Atlanta with, was a born-again Christian, and she had been determined to get me into church. Her persistence had never bothered me. Religion was always of passing interest to me. As a kid in Louisiana, I'd grown up attending Catholic high school. My dad was Jewish, my mother was Episcopalian, and my stint in Los Angeles had brought me in contact with Buddhism, Tibetan mysticism, and Scientology.

But still, I looked at the whole born-again Christian scene with a healthy measure of skepticism. I remember telling my girlfriend as she dragged me into the pew, "If anybody looks at me weird, or if they try to make me sing, talk in tongues, or if I feel uncomfortable in any way, I'm out."

Much to my surprise, the pastor opened his sermon talking about Lance Armstrong. That was someone I could relate to, and it got me to open up a little and listen.

The pastor said Lance started wearing a cross around his

neck in honor of a coworker who, like him, was fighting cancer and also wore a cross. The coworker ended up dying, Lance ended up living, and the crosses they each wore lost much of their significance.

The cross, the pastor concluded, could easily serve as just another symbol for death to Lance. But for Lance and other Christians everywhere, the cross was a symbol of life. I kind of blanked out on everything else he said that day because it was the first time someone in his position wasn't talking *at* me. He was actually talking *to* me. Because of his personalized and respectful communication, the connection he made within me was profound. It made me realize that life wasn't about me. It was about all those who needed what he was telling me.

I left that day with all my prejudices against Christianity in shambles. I wasn't interested in religion, but that pastor's words made me want to learn the truth about Jesus. When I wasn't studying the human body for how to heal my physical condition, I was studying the Bible for a deeper understanding of my purpose as a human.

All this time, I'd been trying to sell myself on the belief that I was important, that I had value. Now I saw the truth: not only was the self-centered life I'd built worthless to me, but it was also worthless to *others*. It represented an act of self-destruction. In life, we all need someone to support us, we all need unconditional love, and we really need someone to lean on in times of need.

I found all of this in my newfound faith in Jesus.

ENTER THE FRANKENBALL

A full year passed. Eventually, I was sitting at my dad's house in Louisiana, talking to him about my plan. All the science I'd researched for the past year had become the framework for a new business idea.

This wasn't a get-rich-or-die-trying scheme, and it wasn't a quest to make a name for myself. This idea was as innovative as my new outlook on life. I'd found something that could help me recover my physical health, and I wanted to share it with others.

The center of the business plan was a ball.

I lovingly called it the Frankenball, constructed of several layers of fabric and rubber. Rolling it against your muscle or joint gave the identical sensation of a manual therapist gently but firmly massaging that spot. I'll be honest: the Frankenball looked weird, but it got the job done!

My dad held the Frankenball in his hands, turning it over, as I explained to him what had been going on with me over the past few years. My body had been breaking down, and the doctors were suggesting multiple sclerosis or fibromyalgia. But I'd researched everything around my symptoms and built my own theory based on six areas of the body that influence biomechanics.

That's how I'd developed this ball, I told him. I'd been using it to massage the muscles, scar tissue, and adhesions that all control how the joints function, and it had actually improved my symptoms. I told him that I was changing physically, mentally, and emotionally. And so much of my transformation was thanks to the Frankenball.

He looked from the ball up at me and raised his eyebrow. "You really think this is a business idea?" he said.

"Nothing exists like this in the world. I have the opportunity—the obligation—to help a whole community of people suffering from the same physical breakdown I experienced. For those people, this ball could change the world. I can even create educational programs all based on the knowledge I'd acquired in the last year."

My dad shook his head and said, as only my dad can, "What is wrong with you? Why don't you get a real job?"

I looked back at him with nothing but love and answered, "That's all I need to hear, Dad. Thanks."

There are so many ways we can look at ourselves as victims if we choose to. My father was a hard man, but he always acted from a place of love. It's just that in that moment with the Frankenball, he didn't know any better.

But I *did* know better, and trusting my gut in that moment, rather than waiting for outside validation, made all the difference in my life from then on. His harsh words propelled me forward from that point, but my own determination brought me success in business.

> You could wait your whole life for outside validation and never get it. What matters in business, and in life, is just one thing: Can you look yourself in the mirror at night and be proud of your work that day? Did you help even one person improve their lives?

THE ANSWER IN WEAKNESS

Having a vision for my new endeavor didn't change the fact that daily life was still a constant struggle. It took me two hours to get out of bed every morning, thanks to the pain that afflicted my muscles and joints. I'd dreamed of training for an IRONMAN race, but I felt *years* away from being IRONMAN-ready.

The only thing that gave me a baseline of self-worth was my growing relationship with Jesus and my desire to model myself after his example.

It struck me that Jesus directed his ministry toward the weakest, lowest members of society. He could have gone after the power brokers of his day—the religious leaders, the Roman rulers—but instead, he sought out people who represented the underbelly of society to offer his message of hope.

In addition, Jesus never "pitched" his message to anybody. He was kind and empathetic, and he offered healing and teaching lessons. He didn't attract people by saying, "I can make you rich," or "I'll make you beautiful and desirable," or even "I can save you from going to Hell."

Instead, he identified their problems at a level deeper than they'd ever recognized. Before the blind man could be healed, he needed to know he was worth fighting for. Before the woman at the well could satisfy her physical thirst, she needed to stop selling herself to men.

This was exactly what I wanted to do with my company: I'd seen enough doctors to know that treating symptoms doesn't cure the disease, but if you don't address the root cause, every symptom you cure will eventually return, often worse than before.

As hard as it was to admit that my body was weak, the more I accurately I identified my weaknesses, the more strategically I was able to use the Frankenball. I would dig into the pain in my body and work it with the ball, eventually melting my symptoms away. Over time, I strengthened, and I eventually regained everything I'd lost.

Then something occurred to me: the same principle might hold true in my personal life. If I began the painful work of digging deep into the root causes of my personal and relational failures, I could fix them.

I realized that I was driven to prove myself successful because so many teachers had given me the message that I'd never amount to anything, or at least I'd struggle trying to keep up with others academically. I failed to recognize that the unique way of thinking that authority figures had chastised me for my entire life was actually one of my greatest strengths.

I compensated by pretending to know everything. All the big disasters in my life, from the movie business to my health to my relationship implosions, happened because I never saw them coming. Believing I had everything figured out kept setting me up for failure.

All along, it had been second nature for me to talk as though I knew everything. So I decided to do the opposite—to make a practice of shutting up and listening.

When I did, an amazing thing happened. I heard my calling for the first time.

THE BIRTH OF TRIGGERPOINT

It turned out that I didn't have to say a word to sell the Frankenball. Although, by this time, I'd advanced my prototype far beyond the Frankenball I'd showed my dad. Now it had the feel of real hands expertly manipulating the fascia.

As I traveled the country talking to people about the ball, it worked as its own infomercial—people constantly stopped me to ask what it was. Rather than answering them with a kinesiology lecture, I turned the question back on them. What ailments were they dealing with? Did they have ongoing pain that troubled them or a physical goal they were struggling to achieve? Then, based on their personal challenges, I showed them how to apply the ball.

From the outset, everything I did at TriggerPoint was focused on our customers, not me.

Amazing connections began to grow out of these interactions. My favorite triathlon shops in town asked if they could carry the ball. I had a conversation at the track with a guy who turned out to be a trademark and corporate attorney, and he loved the ball so much that he did all of

TriggerPoint's legal work for free. People invited me to present TriggerPoint to their networks and invited me to athletic events and trade shows.

These connections gave me a wealth of opportunities to prove the TriggerPoint education. I'd take a volunteer, apply the biomechanical principles I'd learned, and teach a hundred people or more in real time how they could improve their symptoms on their own. Meanwhile, I'd record the encounter so that I could put it on the website, where it could help even more people. There are several ways you can use video as a marketing and educational aid:

HOW TO USE VIDEO AS A MARKETING AND EDUCATIONAL AID

- Record your interactions with customers as a way to teach others online
- Pay a transcription service, such as Rev.com, to transcribe the raw footage
- Break the footage into short videos
- Use the transcriptions as a guideline for future instruction manuals and educational content as well as marketing and ad copy

My success wasn't based on selling a ball or even the education I provided for free. It arose from demystifying people's health for them.

So many of them had been talked down to by doctors, even told that their symptoms were imaginary. It was revolutionary for them to have someone take time to listen while they talked through their pain. By listening, I could truly understand what they needed. I took the complexity of their suffering and made it simple: find your central weakness, gently and consistently work to strengthen it, and all the other symptoms will melt away.

Because I listened to them, they trusted me enough to give our solutions a try. When it worked, it was more than just a cure. It was the fulfillment of the trust they'd chosen to put in me. I understood in a new way what Jesus meant when he told people, "Your faith has healed you." The only difference was that other people's faith in what we were doing was healing me, too.

LIFE RELAUNCHED

When TriggerPoint officially launched, it felt like my life relaunched along with it. I'd built a brand on real impact instead of on hype and posturing. Still, nothing could have prepared me for the immediate attention around TriggerPoint. The overwhelming response our brand received from customers, whose lives we were actively changing, could have taken me right back to the belief I'd started out with: that my successes were what made me important.

Fortunately, the practice of silence had not only transformed how I achieved success, but it also transformed how I handled it going forward. When conflict or confusion arose, instead of ransacking my brain for an answer, I waited for silence to bring the right response out of my past experiences. The more I did this, the lessons I'd learned began to crystallize into short sayings that I could write down, repeat to myself, and offer to others if they needed it.

At first, I called these sayings my mantras. At TriggerPoint, they became known as Cassidyisms. You'll see them throughout this book. They still keep me accountable to what I've learned, and they frame everything I have to pass on.

> If education is a large component of your brand, you need certain scripts for your client-facing team members. Rather than constantly being forced to find the right words to educate each customer, have them follow bullet point steps that allow them to get into the necessary rhythm to allow their authentic passion for the brand shine through. This process allows your team to concentrate on being compassionate and caring for your customers versus just focusing on the sale itself.

No matter how much I've learned, I don't have it all figured out. The one thing I do know is that whatever has made me successful will keep showing up in different areas of my life, pushing me to grow.

In the words of one of Jesus's closest followers, "I am what I am by the grace of God." Real growth happens through service, and service depends on humble silence. Silence is critical for understanding what your business needs from you.

It took losing everything to finally make me silent. When I did stop and listen, I was able to perceive the calling that was there all along: helping people heal their bodies and their minds. It's led me forward ever since and brought me success beyond not only my own dreams but also beyond what anyone ever dreamed was possible for me.

Listening to the pain of others stripped me down to nothing and rebuilt me in His name.

—————— CHAPTER 2 ——————

WHO AND WHAT YOU ARE

In order to be who you want to be tomorrow, you have to accept who you are today.

We've talked about me. Now it's time to talk about you. Just as I had to figure out who and what I was to become the person I wanted to be, you too must figure out who and what you are to build the company into what you want it to be.

As an entrepreneur and leader, you're probably used to promoting your strengths and positive attributes to other people. But to really understand who and what you are, we have to focus in on your problems.

The biggest problem an entrepreneur faces is believing that they can blissfully segment their life. They mistakenly believe that the different sides of their life don't touch each other, that what's happening in one category has no effect on the others.

As a result, when something goes sideways in one part of their life, it never crosses their mind to look for triggers or causes in other parts of their life. Instead, they direct all their mental muscle into fixing each problem within a vacuum.

Entrepreneurs love the adrenaline rush of throwing together a strategy at the last minute. We believe that everything can be solved if we just go harder, longer, stronger.

We're shocked when it doesn't work out that way: when things fall apart, despite our superhuman efforts; when the adrenaline stops flowing; when our natural charisma doesn't draw the same crowd that it used to; when our families and employees are uninspired by our "go big or go home" attitude; when our successes no longer deliver the same euphoric high.

YOU AND YOUR BUSINESS ARE ONE

As an entrepreneur, you can't segment yourself from your business. The various categories of your life do not function independently. They bleed into one another.

When you have trouble communicating at home, you will have trouble communicating at the office. When you let emotion dictate the way that you deal with a situation at work, that same habit will come to bear on your interactions with your partner, your kids, your friends.

This means something much deeper than you being the "face" of your company or even embodying your "lifestyle brand." It means that your professional life and your personal life are inextricable from each other. What happens in one has direct impact on what happens in the other.

If you've picked up this book, it's probably because you've hit a wall. You've been throwing everything you have at a problem with your business, and you still can't move it to the next level. Other parts of your life are falling apart, but you keep giving more to your business because you're convinced that professional success will finally give you the freedom to invest in your personal life—health, relationships, travel, family.

But life doesn't work like that. And neither does business.

PLUMMETING FROM THE PEAK

This chapter is all about you, but in order to illustrate my point, I'm going to tell you a story from my life. The best way to learn is by learning by others' mistakes, right?

I can remember a point in my career when I was very, very tired. I'd been traveling around the world for years. I had alienated my family because I'd put my dedication to TriggerPoint ahead of everything else. I knew I needed to make changes, but I was too tired to weigh my options carefully.

That's when I let my exhaustion make a major decision for me: I resigned as CEO of my company and handed over the reins to someone else.

This new CEO was a good friend of mine. We had deep history together. He was as close to me as a friend can get. I assumed that because I knew him as a friend, I knew him as a businessman. I took it for granted that he would lead the company in the same direction that I would have and that I could get the rest I needed while he did so.

After setting him up as CEO, I left for an amazing vacation that concluded with climbing Mount Kilimanjaro. But after that moment of standing on the peak, thinking I was on top of the world, I came back home and found my own world turned upside down.

Rather than continuing to lead TriggerPoint in the direction I wanted, my new CEO had, in a very few short weeks, changed the DNA of my company.

Coming back to the office and sitting through the first meeting was a living hell. Everything had instantly become about finding the lowest cost of product, creating commodities, and focusing on volume and margins. It was product first, marketing second, and education somewhere trailing behind.

As soon as I left the conference room, my mind took my body into a physical breakdown. I couldn't believe how quickly things could be changed. Was I still not good enough? Was this all my fault? Were my "learning disabilities" keeping me from succeeding?

The thoughts swirling in my head sent my breakdown spiraling, and I was rushed to the hospital with heart attack symptoms.

As I lay there in the hospital, I realized that I couldn't blame anyone but myself. This situation wouldn't have happened if I'd been taking care of things along the way. I always prided myself on my ability to power through the hard yards—my willingness to exhaust myself to make sure things got done—but I had tapped out just when it counted the most. Now I was suffering the consequences, and I didn't know if there was any way to recover.

> Nobody cares that you are tired. Tired is an excuse to cover for the fact that you aren't taking care of yourself. When you make excuses, you become a victim of your own circumstances, which leads to more excuses.

Like me, you might have hired your replacement with the idea that doing so will set you free. However, nobody you hire can support you if you haven't done the hard work of communicating your passion to them. If you don't define their role and set out clear expectations for how they should build process around your passion—if you simply push the chips to their side of the table and say, "Handle this"—there's only one outcome.

They'll sit there for a while, wondering what to do. Then they'll do things their own way, not yours.

I handed over the reins to save my sanity, but in the end, it bit me in the ass. Always take the time to hold people accountable. Don't give them the keys to the car until you know they can drive.

No matter how hard you work, you should never get to the point where you're so tired that you can't lead responsibly. Leaders don't get hall passes. They get held accountable.

Looking back on this situation, it had to happen. I used to hear the phrase "God's got things under control" and think all of that was crap. Of course, now I don't think that.

This was another low in my life. I remember when my dad said to me, "Get all you can get while you can get it. So what's wrong with you? Why don't you get a real job?"

When I started TriggerPoint, my body was at an all-time low. I had no confidence, and then the unbelievable happened: I was rebuilt with a newfound passion (or "born again" as some would say). Now I was dealing with the same adversity again. I was being shut out, controlled, and pushed to my limit. I could have stayed depressed, and I could have been a victim, but rather than allow myself to wallow in pain, I used it to fuel the fire to get off my ass and do something about it. I relit my passion. My wife said to me, "Get off you back and get back in the game!" This time, I had an agenda: I was going to sell the company within the next twelve months. In the process, I doubled down on my faith in Christ and forgave those whom I felt betrayed the foundation TriggerPoint was built on.

PROVERBS 27:23

Be sure you know the condition of your flocks, give careful attention to your herds.

WORKING FOR ACCEPTANCE

It's time to look deeper into what's making you so tired in the first place. There's no question that trying to build a profitable company is hard work. However, there's a difference between hard work and strenuous grinds that last late into the night. If you're pulling one all-nighter after another, subsisting on caffeine and takeout, unable to have a conversation with your friends or spouse without your mind drifting off toward work, it's time to reexamine what you're working so hard *for*.

For a lot of entrepreneurs, their goal isn't something specific, such as turning the balance sheet from red to black. Their ambition is to prove themselves by rising to fulfill impossible expectations so that they'll get the respect they crave.

I know, better than most, what that ambition feels like. Having other people express doubt in me only makes me double down on my resolve. As I shared earlier, my dad's response to my dreams—first acting, then the Frankenball—was the "perfect" motivation to keep me on the path I'd determined to follow.

Strangely, though, achieving success didn't take that chip off my shoulder. Even when my company was selling to many countries around the world, I was still working overtime to make all those who questioned my ability believe in me.

You have to be able to separate that "I'll show everybody" motivation from the way you interact with the people who are actually on your team. When you're feeling frustrated, when the chip on your shoulder starts to weigh heavy, you're most likely to take it out on the people closest to you.

When you spend so much time working, you get closer and closer to your team at your company. Sometimes it gets to the point that you not only spend more time with them than your family, but they wind up feeling like a family too. As a result, it's easy to attack them undeservedly when, really, your frustration is with the world outside of your team. You're just releasing your anger on the people closest to you.

Behavior like this strips away all the confidence your employees have developed in their work skills. The very people who were drawn to you because of your passion become the ones who suffer from your misguided purpose.

It doesn't even matter if you're right about your criticism. If your team tried their hardest and still failed to meet your expectations, there's only one person to blame:

You.

If you didn't prepare your crew by laying out expectations, vision, and a time line, then it's your fault. Being an "eleventh-hour guy" is demeaning to everyone around you. As entrepreneurs, we have a tendency of thinking we know everything and that the people around us should read our minds and know exactly what we want when we want it. But that's just not true. Good communication delivers good results.

Don't get mad at your employees because of your own lack of detail and discipline.

UNDERSTANDING THE PURPOSE-DRIVEN PATH

Once you lose the self-centered "I'll show you" motivation, what's left? At that point, you're like the guy in the revenge movie who, after finally having avenged the wrong done to him, feels lost and adrift in the world. Without that bitterness gnawing at his insides, he has no reason to be great anymore.

The only sustainable motivation is a sense of purpose.

So how do you find the purpose-driven path?

THE PURPOSE-DRIVEN PATH STARTS WITH PEOPLE

You have to know whom you're doing it all for. If you're not doing something that offers positive good to someone in the world—to yourself, if no one else—you'll either burn out fast or never get off the ground.

> **PHILIPPIANS 2:3-4**
>
> Don't be selfish, don't live to make good impressions on others. Be humble, thinking of others as better than yourself. Don't think only of your own affairs but be interested in others, too, and what they are doing.

Doing good doesn't mean you have to be in the nonprofit sector. It doesn't even mean you have to work from purely unselfish motives. My purpose-driven path started with me as my own customer. I was creating a product that would let me heal my own chronic pain.

However, I knew I couldn't be the only person out there suffering from this kind of pain. The more time I spent in the field, the more people I met who were suffering. We were just enough alike to understand each other but different enough to where learning the specifics of their pain gave me the knowledge I needed to create new products. This was what allowed me to build my company.

> It's not what your product is that matters. It's what it does. Find that purpose-driven path for all those who are in need of what you are offering, and you will have more sales than ever before.

Purpose means knowing, specifically and personally, the tangible benefits of your company. You have to know the benefits to your customers and also the benefits to the people who are supporting you professionally and personally. Remember, the two are connected.

THE PURPOSE-DRIVEN PATH IS FULL OF PASSION

Once you know whom your company is serving and how, your passion will stop pushing you toward the kind of behavior that leads to eleventh-hour decisions. Instead, your passion will take over your instincts, leading you to the paths of least resistance between you and your goal.

When you encounter challenges—and you will, even on the purpose-driven path—you don't want to wonder if you chose the wrong path. Knowing that you're on the right track for you is the only thing that gets you through those challenges. More than that, it makes every moment of struggle worth it.

A PURPOSE-DRIVEN PATH MEANS A NEW THOUGHT PROCESS

Purpose changes the yardstick with which you measure your success.

Where you are in life may be ugly. In fact, it almost certainly will be. But the unattractive information that comes from taking a serious reality check is necessary for you as a person and for you in your business.

If you're refusing to accept that you're a poor communicator, then you're setting yourself up for a lifetime of bad communication, both at work and at home. If you're terrible with money but won't acknowledge it, you're setting yourself up for a lifetime of financial problems that will impact everyone who depends on you.

For me at TriggerPoint, I didn't want to acknowledge how weak I was in terms of process. There were lots of fine details of my company that fell on my plate, but they made me uncomfortable and confused. Just like when I was in school, I felt like I had to convince everyone that I knew what I was doing, or else they'd see through me and think I was stupid. That fear kept me from taking an accurate assessment of reality.

In general, people are afraid of where they are in their lives: they're afraid of admitting they don't know everything about their business, and they're afraid of the responsibility that reality demands of them. As a result, they hide from the truth so much that they no longer see reality as it is.

> Do you know how many famous people are actually very lonely? They live a famous life—always surrounded by people—with material wealth thrown at them from every direction, yet they no longer know who the heck they are. Depression is a part of their DNA because they are so lost they don't remember what truly makes them happy. They dictate what they want their life to be, but what happens when they reach a point where they need a team? Typically, they look around and see the truth: they are all alone. That's what happens when you don't constantly take stock of reality.

At the gym, people commonly neglect their warm-up. They're so impatient to jump into the workout that they don't take the time to prepare. But if you don't do the warm-up, you're setting yourself up to fail the workout, whether through injury or suboptimal results.

Reality checks work the same way. They don't look glamorous; nobody will congratulate you for doing them. But as we've seen, they're essential to accomplishing the good in the world that your company exists to do.

A REALITY CHECK PROCESS
TO MINIMIZE CONFLICT

1. Stop

This is the hardest part of a reality check—stopping what you're doing long enough to really take in the situation.

2. Look

Step out of the situation and observe everyone and everything in it. Start with the expressions on their faces and their body language. Is everyone tired, excited, happy, frustrated? These are good indicators of how the interaction is going.

3. Listen

Review what's been said by the people in the situation (if you even know what it was). Remove the emotion, the defensiveness, the eagerness to be right from the equation, and really examine the words. (I know removing the emotion from a passionate person is like removing Excel from an operations professional. But just do it. You'll be fine.)

4. Assess

Once you've taken in the information, describe that reality back to yourself. Are you happy, sad, frustrated, excited? Are you the one causing frustration for those who are frustrated? In other words, are you the bottle-neck in the equation? What is the overall perspective, and can you redefine the thought process of those involved by talking to them the same way you want to be talked to?

If the assessment is that you are unhappy, ask whether your business is what it should be in your life, or if it has taken on a different role? Are your employees actively engaged in your company's mission, or do they lack direction?

In order to know where you are, you've got to always be stopping, looking, listening, and assessing not only the situation but also yourself.

If you don't do all of these actions, you may find yourself beating your head against the same wall every day. If you are the problem and you're willing to change, fantastic. If you're not willing to change, you have to surround yourself with people you can openly communicate with.

Reality checks allow you to articulate problems and share them with people who can offer you the insight you need. Remember, you're not an anomaly. At the end of the day, there are others who have gone through whatever it is that you're going through.

Being on the purpose-driven path means not resting until you find those people. It means not only admitting your issues but also implementing advice from the team you've surrounded yourself with.

Even if it costs you your pride.

DON'T WAIT FOR TRANSFORMATION

I hear it from entrepreneurs all the time: "Once I get this business up and running, things will be really different.

I'll finally have all these things that I've always wanted in life. I'll finally be happy."

Some call that magical thinking. I call it bullshit. Happiness based on a dream of the future isn't happiness. Having an idea of happiness isn't fulfilling. Your present reality is what makes you really happy. Period.

If you're reading this book expecting it to transform you, I've got bad news: you're headed for failure. I can't force you to do anything. You have to want to make change.

At best, I can provide you with a set of tools, but tools can't help you unless you use them. Even if I write a book that makes everything in your business crystal clear, the fix will not be quick. There's work to be put in, even once everything makes sense. You're the only one who can change everything.

CHAPTER 3

WORK LIFE BALANCE IS SOMETHING YOU EARN

Don't undervalue who and what you are.

TriggerPoint grew at an amazing pace. We had an office, a dedicated workforce, an established brand, a ground-breaking marketing strategy, and a steadily growing profit margin. However, I'd begun to notice that my ass was spending a lot more time in a chair than it did on a bike. Running a successful fitness company didn't mean fitness would just show up in my life.

At the same time, I saw that my employees were working just as hard as I was. They were putting in the same sacrifices to serve TriggerPoint's vision, and I wanted to make that work-life balance easy for them too.

> Fortunately, I had the resources to make balance easier. First, I put a CrossFit gym into TriggerPoint's office. Next, I started bringing in healthy food for everybody.
>
> Looking back, I wish I'd done more. I wish I'd been as aware of other imbalances in my life as I was of the physical imbalance. I wish that I had the discipline to create those balances ahead of time, instead of letting them go for so long.

THE MYTH OF BALANCE

Balance is a big buzzword these days. Everybody wants this thing called *work-life balance*. I've seen it mentioned as a reason that people quit their corporate jobs and strike out on the entrepreneurial trail. They'll claim that the nine-to-five grind was sucking their soul, that they needed to create something that gave them freedom and flexibility to enjoy their life and find fulfillment.

That kind of rhetoric makes me laugh. The entrepreneurs I know are some of the *least* balanced people you'll ever meet.

Work-life balance is something you earn. You don't just fall into it as a result of starting your own business. Sure, when you own your own business, you can do whatever the hell you want, but what you don't realize before you start your business is that entrepreneurship changes what you *want* to do.

Where you used to plan vacations, count on time off for holidays, and forgot about your job as soon as you walked out the door at six o'clock, now you're connected to your phone or laptop no matter where you are. The ability to schedule anything anytime ends up making your schedule more packed, not less.

Unless, of course, you practice the discipline to remain balanced.

Technology makes it easy to divide your entire day into a set of timers. This is what I did. At two o'clock, I went for a run. At three o'clock, I returned emails. At four o'clock, I went home to make out with my wife. At five o'clock, I spent time meditating and giving thanks for everything I had.

You know who else does that? Almost no one, especially not entrepreneurs.

They wake up supermotivated to make their business succeed but completely clueless about what specific tasks will achieve that success. They go about their day with no personal intention or purpose, responding to other people's expectations. The craziest part is that they expect to come out the other end of the day feeling good about what they've done.

Ask any professional athlete how well time management works, and they'll tell you there's no way they could succeed with no time discipline. Contrary to what you might imagine, these people who look like beasts do not naturally drift onto the track or the weight room as soon as they wake up.

When they're in training for a competition, everything about their life is preplanned and programmed beyond the possibility of error. As a result of this discipline, they don't have to wonder how many calories to eat at each meal or whether they should spend the day on their sport, cross-training, or allowing their muscles to rest and recover. Discipline is what enables them to develop the physical and mental balance required for greatness in any sport.

If you're intent on achieving greatness in your career or business, you must practice discipline.

HIRE FOR YOUR WEAKNESSES

Don't struggle with doing what you can't do. Thrive at doing what you can do.

It's important to be real with yourself about your bandwidth. When you're running a company, you can't expect yourself to manage everything in your life at the highest level of performance.

We as entrepreneurs don't like to be vulnerable. We like acting as though our dysfunctions make us badass and help define our brand. But over time, these habits turn into liabilities for a person or a company that wants to grow and live to a ripe old age.

Don't take for granted your desire to be healthy, to grow, and to mature. When something's not right in your body or brain, don't waste valuable time trying to self-diagnose. Get someone to help you fix it, whether it's a marriage counselor, a massage therapist, or a business mentor. Bring in specialists who can strengthen the balance of your life for you so that you can give every area of your life the full focus it deserves.

When you're at work, give everything to your business. When you're at home, give everything to your family. When you're working out, give everything to the machine or the exercise. When you're engaging in your spiritual practice, give everything to your faith.

The great thing about discipline is that it lets you change who and what you are. Memories are short—other people's and your own. Once you've implemented your new discipline ten to twelve times, it becomes a rote behavior. You barely have to think about it anymore. It becomes just who you are. It doesn't take much longer for other people to start recognizing you as that disciplined person as well.

USE YOUR TIME WISELY

There are only twenty-four hours in a day. Hire around all your weaknesses. Find people who are more educated than you in your space and collaborate with them in the same "with, not for" mentality.

In the end, you'll have created a team around you who all believe in the same mission. By believing in the same thing as you, they can help you get to the next level.

I've been surprised to find that the more collaborative I am, the more I enjoy my work. The times that I tried to retain control of everything, held back from sharing my knowledge in fear that people would screw it up, guess what? They screwed it up anyway. They could never meet my expectations *because I didn't communicate my expectations.* Instead of a group of people striving for the same mission, all I created was a melting pot for conflict and disappointment.

At the inception of your company, you're rich on time and poor in finances. There's nothing you can do about it except keep working in hopes that the proportion balances out over time—that you make more money so you don't have to keep pulling those twenty-hour days.

As your company grows, that proportion does shift. However, if you're like a lot of entrepreneurs, you remain stuck in the "not enough money" mindset.

You have to take a reality check and realize that you need to buy back some time. Part of that investment is hiring the right people. The key here is hiring for consistency in your life, especially where things don't come easily to you.

If you find it hard to remember things such as regular date nights or planning a family vacation, hire a part-time nanny who will come in once a week, and engage a travel agent who will do the vacation planning for you.

If you want to really succeed in bringing balance back to your life, consider hiring for even the things you do know about. For example, even though I had expertise in fitness and athletics, as my company grew I still hired a personal trainer to help me get back in shape. That way, I didn't have to spend the time planning out my workout. I just walked into the gym and did what my trainer told me to do. It felt great to turn my brain off and allow somebody else's expertise to take over that area of my life.

BUYING BACK TIME

There is nothing wrong with spending money to make your life a little more efficient. Once you can afford it, hire someone to cut your grass. It's a waste of time if you do it while working your ass off. Hire someone to give you a massage. You're not going to get on the ground and roll out if you're cranking hours at the office.

This is not a waste of dollars; these are dollars very well spent.

I used to have my lunch brought in, coffee delivered, date night scheduled, flight schedules programmed into my phone, folders for travel, drivers for commuting (when I didn't know where I was), and I wore the same thing almost every day when growing Trigger-Point. There are many who would say that I'm OCD, ADD, ADHD, and I say, "Thank you." I am all of those things, and that's why paying for the right things feels good. I truly needed the help to be successful.

HOW TO FIND BALANCE IN YOUR COMPANY

- If you're spending months trying to crack into a market that won't budge, ask yourself why. Is it good for the business, or are you just trying to prove something?

- If you're considering a major new product line, will it help your business achieve its potential for greatness, or are you simply trying to be good at everything?

- How many products/services do you offer as a business? Which ones are making money and which ones are wasting time? Are they quality products with a healthy margin, or are they outdated, taking the company focus in the wrong direction?

- More is not better. Narrow the product offering and do a great job, versus expanding the product offering and offering only a marginal experience.

PARALYSIS BY ANALYSIS

You can overanalyze anything. When your mind encounters uncertainty or fear, it turns the situation into a complex knot of variables that keep you endlessly thinking through the situation and never doing anything to change it. I call this *paralysis by analysis*, and most of the time, all it does is delay your decision until the eleventh hour, when you're out of time.

At that point, you undermine the confidence of everyone who works with you and usually end up making a move borne of desperation, one that compromises the very goal you intended to achieve.

There's a simple solution to paralysis by analysis. Instead of letting your mind get tangled up in complexity, you can simply trust your gut. It's unbelievable how your gut is typically right.

Think about when you've been in a bad situation. Usually, it starts out good. You wouldn't put yourself in a bad situation on purpose. But then your gut starts sending you warning signals. *Something's not right here. Get out while you still can.*

Immediately, though, your brain tries to override it. It's that paralysis by analysis. Your brain tries talking you into staying where you are in order to not take the risk of changing what you're doing.

Meanwhile, your gut is telling you the reality of the situation. If you let it lead you, you might never know what it saved you from, but if you ignore it, you'll end up spending a lot of time afterward wishing that you'd gone the simple route and trusted your gut.

GIVE CHANGE THE TIME IT DESERVES

We've already talked about how to make balance simple. Instead of trying to handle all the details of your life individually, you program them into your schedule, create habits out of them, and find people who can support you in making sure those disciplines get executed.

The same goes for each individual area of your business. Branding, marketing, sales, product, and of course, operations and administration—all of these fall into place when you *strip away the complexity and focus on simplicity.*

Every area of your business is made up of organizational procedures. These procedures are to your business what joints and fascia are to your body—they allow it to move forward in an intentional direction, with varying degrees of speed and efficiency.

You need healthy, high-functioning organizational procedures to move forward over the long haul. At the same time, you need purpose to determine which direction constitutes "forward."

Most entrepreneurs are nonlinear thinkers. It comes with the territory of being a visionary. You imagine the company you want to build and expect everyone you hire to intuitively understand what you have in mind. If you do acknowledge the need for processes and even go through the trials and tribulations of creating that process—an exhausting labor for many entrepreneurs—you feel entitled to instant implementation.

You forget that even the best processes don't deliver results overnight.

Ultimately, what it really requires is respect. You have to respect the process itself and allow it to build results over time, which is the only way a process works. You must also respect the people implementing the process and the situation into which you've introduced it.

CHAPTER 4

COMMUNICATION IS MORE THAN WORDS— IT'S YOUR CORE

A crucial part of leading people in creating habits is making sure they understand the why behind those habits—not just the big-picture why of your organization but also the individual why of their role. In other words, they need to clearly understand the expectations you have for them in their role.

Structure and discipline are imperative to have others meet your expectation. But without one core component, all the structure and discipline in the world won't help your employees succeed in the role you've given them.

The missing link is communication.

At TriggerPoint, we talk a lot about core-to-extremity movements. These are the most powerful movements you can make as an athlete. Your arms and legs, the extremities, are what deliver the effect in most sporting events. But limiting those movements to just your arm or just your leg doesn't deliver nearly as much power as if you start the movement from your core.

Core-to-extremity movements work a lot like a slingshot. You pull back the center, and as you let go, it can throw an object forward with incredible torque and force. Any athlete in any sport knows that they move faster through this core-to-extremity movement.

It's also a great way to think about how your business operates. You're probably used to hearing terms such as *core values* and *core cultural components*. Those are at the core of your business much the same way your heart and lungs are at the core of your body. They are important for keeping your business alive. But when I talk about the core of your company, I'm not referring to your core values.

I'm referring to the way you get that value into your customers' heads and hands.

Back when I was peddling my Frankenball around the

country, one-on-one communication was everything to me. If I could communicate my message clearly and authentically—that we were in the business of empowering people to do things they never thought possible—I could connect to someone.

If I could connect to just one person, I could connect with the crowd listening in. If I could connect with that crowd, I could make sure that they went home with the free educational content we provided. Eventually, it brought them back for more because they knew they could trust us to help them become who and what they wanted to be.

As we grew, that messaging went out to individuals, then to cities, and then to one country after another. At our peak, we were reaching eighty-six countries around the world, all from this little office of forty-something people in Austin, Texas.

But to keep that message strong, I had to make sure that the core communication in my company remained strong. This meant ensuring that I was communicating TriggerPoint's values to my employees so that they could relay the message consistently in their various roles. This consistent message was the uniting concept that allowed them to work independently yet as one.

If the core values of your company are not leading you

toward your vision, both within your office walls and outside of them, your company's extremities will be dysfunctional. Many times, that dysfunction will show up at the moment of contact with the customer.

WORK AS A JOYFUL PART OF LIFE

It makes you understand why companies such as Google, Facebook, or Zappos have done so well. The joy that they have in their office ends up being the same joy that's shared with the customer. Hundreds of different people within this company are linked together in creating an experience for the customer. If it went wrong at any point in the chain, the customer might get a bad experience. But they don't.

Customers of these companies routinely report feeling special, taken care of as if they are a VIP. That tells you that these companies' core values are so strong and the discipline of sharing them is so regimented that the employee mindset is uniformly awesome. They feel valued; they feel recognized; they feel like they are seen and treated as a quality person. When you feel this way, it's easy to pass on that same feeling to the customer. You don't even have to think about it.

CAREFUL COMMUNICATIONS

From a business standpoint, the extremities are anything that takes your company "out of the office," as it were. That means product, branding, marketing, and sales. You can build the greatest company culture in the world and have your office running like a well-oiled machine, but if you haven't spent quality time defining your expectations for how those extremities will perform, you're setting them up for failure.

Looking back, I see what I ought to have done at TriggerPoint: less coaching, more asking for feedback; less money spent on lunches, more time spent listening.

To get your core working efficiently, it's merely a matter of implementing some simple disciplines.

STOP

Stop assuming you know who and what your employees are. Sit down with your employees in a neutral setting—over lunch, before or after a meeting—and get to know them. Seek to understand why they are sitting in that chair in your office. Start cultivating a genuine interest in helping them achieve their goals and dreams. Be more interested in who they are than what they can do for you.

LOOK

When you're examining an employee's performance, don't just compare it to what you had in your mind. Consider what structures and processes are in place (or *aren't* in place) to guide their performance. Pay attention to *how* they do the work they're doing. If they demonstrate passion in their performance, you're lucky to have them.

LISTEN

The amount of time you spend coaching an employee should be matched by the amount of time you spend listening to them. Make it safe for them to be honest about you and the company. Don't just ask for their feedback; receive it with trust. Remember, they chose to work with your company, so they must have an investment in helping you achieve your goals.

REALITY CHECK

Going through the motions won't cut it. You have to bring your own core strength, based on who and what you are, to the "stop, look, and listen" process. Before you attempt to communicate with others, communicate honestly with yourself. Take that reality check and recognize that you're lucky to have the workforce that you do. These are the people you chose to share your passion and serve your company's mission of doing good in the world.

If you do these things with your employees, you'll be amazed. They will give you everything.

WHAT MILLENNIALS HAVE RIGHT

Senior executives like to rag on millennials for wanting too many feel-good vibes from their workplace.

The truth is that millennials are onto something. Many of us, especially in the start-up world, spend more time with our coworkers than we do with our actual families. It really shouldn't be that way, but it makes sense.

The workforce is growing with people who value meaningful work over money. They don't take jobs solely for the sake of a good starting salary, a strong benefits package, or even the likelihood of job security. They want to spend their working hours as part of a community with common values and a mission that they are passionate about.

A company that employs people like this can't help but function like a family.

In many ways, a millennial employee is looking in the workplace for things that their actual family didn't give them. The average millennial grew up as a latchkey kid, possibly splitting his or her life between the two homes of divorced parents. They got a lot of gifts but not so much quality time. They were given blue ribbons for participation, but they weren't taught and guided in overcoming challenges to achieve excellence.

This desire for a family-like culture is an amazing opportunity for you as an employer. A workforce built on close, trusting relationships means tighter organization, more honest communication, intrinsic motivation born of collective passion for each other's well-being.

It's possible for companies to take this family atmosphere to an unholy extreme. We all know how families, despite their close bonds, can take one another for granted. They might take out emotions on each other with words that they can't take back.

This is where discipline comes in. As a leader, you're effectively serving as a parent. You're giving high fives, even hugs, but you're also holding everyone to a high standard of respect and communication. You're showing personal interest and care, but you're doing it by setting clear expectations. You're allowing for the times when people have a bad day, but you're also creating processes that guard against them creating a pattern out of that bad day.

By applying the discipline needed to correct bad habits and create daily rituals that cultivate success, you're developing balance within those bonds. You're creating a situation where the core strength emanates seamlessly out to the extremities, accomplishing your common purpose and fulfilling your shared passion.

If you find yourself resisting this model, it's time to get over it. In 2020, 75 percent of the global workforce will be millennials. Already, the greatest amount of wealth in our world is generated by people who are thirty-five and under. These workers are demanding a huge transformation in the way corporate structures are defined. You can resist it for only so long. If you only care about what they can do for you, they will quit or drive you crazy.

The complexity of their emotion requires a simple solution: they just want to know that you care about them, that they matter to you, that you value and even enjoy them for who they are.

I get that this is difficult for the type-A CEO. Believe me, I was brought up by baby boomers. I was taught to keep my head down, work hard, and not expect any rewards beyond money and, maybe eventually, power. Those were the only two currencies that professionals had respect for.

Those things haven't lost their clout completely, but they are being balanced out by the upcoming workforce's value for relationships and the desire to make a difference.

So get over yourself. Be genuinely interested in who and what your employees are, and it's amazing what you can get out of them, both professionally and personally.

CONSULTANTS INFLUENCE EVERYTHING YET ARE RESPONSIBLE FOR NOTHING

A classic move for company leaders who aren't willing to adapt their own style is to hire consultants to come in and fix the dysfunction. They miss the whole point that they are marinating in a culture they've created. They think that everyone else is the problem, and the quick, cost-effective solution is to bring in an outside "expert" who can whip the place into shape.

In my experience, consultants do a lot more harm than good. Every short-term consultant I've ever hired just created more chaos than was there when they showed up.

Consultants influence everything yet are responsible for nothing. They come in, and they tell you all the problems that you have, but they're not able to fix them because they're not willing to put the time and effort into fixing them. Why should they be?

Your workforce's relationships aren't their relationships. Your company's purpose is not their purpose. Consultants show up and apply an objective set of theories to you, but because those theories have no reference to your company's history, mission, and values, they are, in most cases, objectively wrong.

As a result, the presence of a consultant can disrupt the

core of your business. If you tell them your marketing department isn't performing, you can be sure that they will go in and completely change it. In their wake will be a confused staff who are now trying to reconcile the newly introduced processes to their vague understanding of your poorly communicated expectations.

In other words, you now have an added layer of stress to your existing dysfunction. That added stress can be the exact thing that breaks an employee, a department, even an entire company.

In my experience, you're better off doing the work of identifying your problem areas and enlisting people experienced in your company to help you treat the problem through implementing discipline.

IF YOU TREAT THE PROBLEM, THE SYMPTOMS GO AWAY

It may be raw and uncomfortable; in fact, it almost certainly will be. But it will be more effective than continuing to address the symptoms of the problem that you've created through lack of discipline.

It's unbelievably painful to admit that you aren't the best at everything in your own company. Once you make this realization, you're faced with a choice: you can allow your weaknesses to define you, or you can surround yourself with people who strengthen your weaknesses.

If you surround yourself with those people and submit to being raw and vulnerable with them about your weaknesses, you'll have the greatest asset any company founder can ask for: motivated people.

It's time to ask yourself why you started your company in the first place: Did you do it to make people appreciate and admire you? Or did you start this company to do some good in the world?

If you are truly dedicated to improving the world, you have to allow the company to grow bigger than you.

I want to be clear: if you read this book, apply the principles, and truly believe in who and what you are, I don't believe that you should ever remove yourself as the CEO of the company.

It all goes back to balance. Find help to strengthen your weaknesses, but still maintain balance by keeping control of the company.

This doesn't mean you have to double-check everything, swoop in at the eleventh hour, or worry about not being the company you originally set out to create. A great leader leads by setting expectations, communicating a vision, and trusting in his team. If you do all those things, you will always be the visionary leader of your company.

CHAPTER 5

TO BE WHO YOU WANT TO BE IN LIFE, YOU NEED TO ACCEPT WHO YOU ARE TODAY

What you tolerate, you accept.

If you tolerate being a victim, you'll always be a victim. If you tolerate what your parents or a teacher said to you as a child, you will always be a by-product of their perception. A boss who hates you, an employee who takes advantage of you, a neighbor who always puts his trash can in front of your driveway—why do we tolerate these things?

Because it feels safer than standing up and saying no.

Most people will tolerate just about anything as long as they feel safe. That means they will get into average relationships, they'll get into average jobs, design their life around average desires. No great risks, but no great joy either. Maybe it's satisfying to them. I see it as sad. I believe you should always want more than what you have today.

For years, I tolerated people saying I was dumb, that I couldn't perform at a university level, that I'd never have financial independence, or that I'd always be codependent on relationships and parental guidance. It took me a long time to realize that by tolerating their words, I'd accepted them as part of my identity.

That realization was what allowed me to say, "Screw it. I'm not going to be that person anymore. I'm choosing to risk everything in order to live my own life."

In my family's eyes, I was throwing away all the financial security that came with following in their footsteps. But by the time I was ready to start TriggerPoint, I was coming into it as a whole person with a purpose-driven path that I could translate into a global business.

Making change doesn't mean you have to upend your entire life in one go. But you do have to make a conscious choice to accept what you've been passively accepting through toleration.

Realizing who and what I was allowed me to transform my life into a giving role. I had a very clear definition of the person who was in need of what I created with TriggerPoint. I knew how to communicate to that person because that person *was* me. I was talking to myself.

A NEW PERSPECTIVE

Companies fail when they neglect the simple fact that the customer is a person, and that person has a real problem that they need solved. That said, in order to become successful in your business and in life, you must understand how important it is to accept who *you* are today before you can accept who your customer is.

START OFF BY ASKING YOURSELF THESE QUESTIONS:

1. Who are you?

Am I really living the life that makes me happy? When I shut my eyes and fall into a dream, do I see myself in the dream that is imitating my life, or am I doing something else? Am I happy, sad, angry, frustrated? Do I blame others versus taking the blame? Do I blame myself so much so that I don't feel threatened by others?

2. Where are you?

Am I where I am supposed to be in life, in my job, in my career? Is this where I envisioned myself as a kid? Am I clean and kept, or dirty and a slob?

3. Why are you?

The big question is, why am I who I am? Am I proud of me? Will I stand up for me? Am I a victim or an advocate? Did someone hurt me? Am I living out someone else's life, or am I living out my life?

If you're like most people, you have an inner dialogue of goals running through your head throughout the day. To turn those dreams into goals, you've got to say them out loud. To be clear, I *am* recommending talking to yourself throughout the day. Better still, look at yourself in the mirror while doing so.

This simple switch—speaking your *who* and *what* out loud—turns them into goals. It forces you to confront your reality, and ask yourself if you really want to make a change.

People fear speaking aloud what they really feel, even to themselves. But like it or not, that's who you are. Looking in yourself in the mirror and being vulnerable lets you know that there is nothing wrong with you that you don't have the power to change. It's up to you whether you use that vulnerable reality as a vehicle to success or as the reason never to pursue success. Either way, at least you've made a conscious choice.

LEARNING A NEW LANGUAGE

Another factor was that modes of communication were changing rapidly just at the time I started hiring for TriggerPoint. The new reality of texting, email, and social media messaging was a whole new language that I had to build into my communication pathway.

I never thought about how the same words I said in person could sound completely different when they came via text message. I never considered how emotion and tone didn't translate through electronic communication. I thought I was being direct and to the point. Instead, I was coming off as terse, unapproachable, and uncaring—the opposite of who and what I wanted my business to be.

I wanted to be caring and communicative, as a person and as a company leader. But I didn't reflect as hard as I should have on this aspect of my business. I knew my business existed to provide care for people who were suffering, but I wasn't paying attention to the way my employees were suffering.

Honestly, if I had seen this, I would have resolved to make changes. But I know that it would have been difficult for me. I was used to communicating in one way, and it wasn't working. It goes back to the Cassidyism: "What you tolerate, you accept." By continuing to tolerate my own bad communication, I was accepting a dysfunction within my company. No matter how often I said I wanted to fix that dysfunction, I ultimately wasn't willing to be vulnerable enough to admit that I didn't know how.

Here's the truth I learned later: it's OK not to know how. It's as good a place as any to start from. The key is not tolerating what you claim not to accept.

The entrepreneur mindset is that the harder you work, the more people will appreciate you. But it's just not true. The harder you work, the harder it is for you to relate to anyone who doesn't work as hard as you do.

DON'T FIGHT YOUR DNA

Personally, I find it hard to relate to people who don't work hard. I come at things from an athlete's mentality. I'd rather work my ass off trying and failing than never trying at all. My approach is to develop discipline and drive by any tactics necessary.

But as a business owner, you *have* to relate to people who

view success differently from how you do. You need their talents, their youthful insight, and yes, even their different perspective to build your business to what you want it to be.

You have to know the DNA of your business, who and what it is made of, and learn how to relate to it in a way that gets you the results you want. You have to change the way you do things if you want your team to understand the direction, grasp the vision, and adopt the focus you're setting for them. Otherwise, you're all on your own.

In order to execute this on a company-wide level, you have to get the original employees to work in sync with the new employees. I won't sugarcoat it. It's very hard. You'll be learning at the same time that you are implementing. You just have to be very patient with everyone. But if you've learned good communication skills by this point, you'll be able to clearly communicate your vision and lay the path down with both old and new in your employment pool.

In all seriousness, the old think they know better and are lazy, while the new are typically firing on all cylinders, trying to prove that they know everything. Be patient, stay true to the company and brand, focus on the end consumer, and refrain from calling out anyone in front of anyone else.

Once you create bad blood with the old or new, it will always be there. It's very hard to rid the inner office animosity and anxiety. Blending the old and new is something that you've got to do slowly, gracefully, and respectfully.

THE WHO AND WHAT OF YOUR BRAND

Your strongest branding happens through your employees. If they love who and what the brand is, they will take it out into the world on their own initiative. They will be living the meaning it has to them, and the more they do this, the more recognizable the brand will become.

Once you have the luxury of just putting your logo on something and instantly communicating who and what your company is, you've won. That is the holy grail of branding.

Again, you don't get there overnight. A thriving brand strategy doesn't just happen. You must lead your company in asking the hard questions.

> ### QUESTIONS TO ASK YOURSELF ABOUT YOUR BRAND
>
> - Do *you* understand who and what your brand is?
> - Are you communicating it authentically, or are you just using buzzwords to fill in the gaps?
> - Does your mark value simplicity over complexity?
> - Are your employees drawn to your brand? (e.g., Do they wear it all the time? Do they use it as part of their personal identity?)
> - Are you living your brand as well as wearing it?
> - Does your brand generate curiosity or confusion?

THE WHO AND WHAT OF YOUR MARKETING

Today's consumer can smell inauthenticity a mile away. While they might sometimes fall for the "quick fix" or the cheap option, they'll only do that until they find a brand that they can have a relationship with. Remember, when you give people what they want, they'll go away and never come back. But if you give them what they need, they'll always come back for more.

If you'll do the hard work to realize what your brand is and why it needs to exist, you'll have a message that will draw the market to you. No attention-grabbing ploys needed.

One of the simplest ways to convey this message is by offering education to your customers. This is what I call *marketing with integrity*. It's now more widely known as content marketing.

If you want your company to stand the test of time, your marketing has to show your customer that there is a purpose-driven path behind your products. You can't simply throw the product on the shelf and rely on catchy gimmicks to sell it. You need to explain to that person why and how they should use it.

This tactic won't make your company money right away, and that tends to scare people off. In a recent training I gave to an executive team, when I explained to them about education marketing, they had immediate objections.

"We can't just give the customer knowledge to take home and use on their own," they said. "What if they never come back to buy our product?"

I had to point out how insecure that statement made them sound. Did they even believe that their product needed to exist? If so, they had nothing to be afraid of.

"The more you provide to the customer to do on their own," I told them, "the more often they'll come back to you."

Marketing with integrity sets your brand on a foundation of relevance. It will keep your team passionately engaged on your brand's behalf by connecting with their desire for purposeful work. This passion and integrity will translate to a long-lasting relationship with the end consumer. They'll see that you've gone the extra mile, and they'll trust you because of it.

THE WHO AND WHAT OF YOUR PRODUCT

If you have found yourself holding a shiny new product and frustrated because no one is buying it, it's time to ask yourself some questions.

"What's wrong with my marketing?" is where most people would start. But that doesn't go deep enough.

"What's wrong with my product?" is a deeper place to begin questioning. But again, you have to go deeper than that.

QUESTIONS TO ASK YOURSELF ABOUT YOUR PRODUCT

- What am I doing for my customer? Am I giving them what they need or what they want? Am I treating them the way I want to be treated by other companies? Is my company 80 percent education and 20 percent marketing?

- How will this product help them? Am I educating the customer on how the product provides the desired lifestyle, or am I just educating them on how to use the product? To help someone is to enhance their quality of life. Are you doing that and, if so, how?

- What are the strengths and weaknesses of my product? You may have to admit that this product or service isn't right for everyone. That's OK. This builds trust with potential customers.

The real place to start when nobody's buying your product is, "What's wrong with me?"

People usually think of product and sales as something that precedes marketing. You create the product, you devise the sales strategy, and then you overlay a marketing campaign onto it as necessary.

But if you're entering the market with integrity, product and sales are the final step in the queue. Product and sales are the by-products of marketing. Before your product can become what you want it to be, you have to accept who you are today. Your education-based marketing will reveal where a product is truly required to make your information as effective as it can be. This is where you find the game-changing opportunities.

Anything less than a game-changing opportunity means you're playing by the existing rules. Instead of creating a product that needs to exist, you end up with a me-too product—another version of someone else's innovation.

For founders who are merely after getting a share of a burgeoning market, a me-too product is enough. If that's you—if money and sales are your end game—this book is probably not for you.

A focus on market share is incompatible with real care for the customer. When your vision is to do good in the world, you won't be satisfied with anything short of being disruptive. If you are setting out to redefine an industry, the product is secondary to the outcome.

Don't misunderstand. The product has to be great, and you must think through every aspect of how the end consumer will feel, experience, and react once the product is in their hands. But in all your communication with the customer, you have to put far more emphasis on the outcome than on the product.

REALITY CHECK—PLANTAR FASCIITIS

In 2007, TriggerPoint was growing every day, doing about $5 million per year in sales. We had a slew of products that we packaged into different kits for addressing various conditions and physical issues. It was a great way to build a brand. One kit that I was particularly excited about was built to address plantar fasciitis, a pain in the bottom of the foot that affects runners in particular.

A glance into the market around plantar fasciitis revealed a billion-dollar industry. There were hundreds of different products—shoes, inserts, straps, braces, socks, all made to address the pain and dysfunction caused by this condition. I took one look at that market and said to my team, "You know what? It's time to be disruptive again."

At TriggerPoint, I was fortunate to have worked with many people around the world with plantar fasciitis. I'd already created an educational program that allowed customers to eliminate plantar fasciitis in as little as a day. I knew that whereas physical therapists and other practitioners focused on the bottom of the foot, where the pain of plantar fasciitis manifests, the real problem lies with the muscle at the posterior lower leg.

Other people were selling the outcome of the product based on something they didn't know. I did know the root cause, but I also knew that it would take a lot of time and effort to educate the market around our program.

TriggerPoint's growth trajectory was built on changing the thought process around physical dysfunction. Eighty percent of our marketing was education based, while the other 20 percent was in promotion.

But this time, I got impatient.

I saw the wide-open opportunity for disruption and decided to just go after it. We still educated people about the root cause of plantar fasciitis, showing them strategies for addressing it and offering our product kit as a tool for implementing those strategies. But now I said, "F$#k it. Let's go big. Let's go against all the big players in the market. Let's go to SkyMall."

We were still doing education-based marketing on our plantar fasciitis kit but in this mainstream channel. We channeled our 80 percent education, 20 percent marketing approach to the average Joe sitting on an airplane. And it worked! Just three months after launching our plantar fasciitis kit, we'd done about $300,000 in sales, thanks mainly to direct marketing.

Because our product worked so well, it made us a global sensation. It was enough to turn the heads of globetrotters on every airline. I remember thinking, *This is amazing!* This made me realize that the world needed what I had. Education is marketing with integrity. The world really just wants to know the why, and if you can provide it to them, they will buy!

It was amazing, right up until the Food and Drug Administration contacted me and shut my business down. They said we couldn't brand with physical health claims that they hadn't approved. Overnight, customs began quarantining all the product we'd shipped—not just the plantar fasciitis kit but everything with the TriggerPoint mark on it. Our sales were frozen. We couldn't even ship standing orders. We spent December 2008 contacting customers to explain why they wouldn't be receiving their purchases in time for the holidays.

I blew through a quarter of a million dollars trying to fix this problem and learned the hard way that you don't get in a pissing match with the government.

I argued that plantar fasciitis was not a disease but rather a condition. They said it didn't matter. We couldn't use the word *treat* anywhere in our marketing. We couldn't ship any product until we rebranded everything, from our website on down.

Looking back, I can see where we went wrong. It wasn't

that I was greedy; it was that we were a little too bliss-fully ignorant. We had stayed under the radar for so long because one of my tactics was to appear small but continue to grow as big as possible while still main-taining the homegrown boutique feel for as long as we could. What I failed to realize was that once we went into SkyMall, we were marketing to the masses, and the big boys in the plantar fasciitis industry caught wind. Regardless of who turned the Food and Drug Admin-istration onto us, this was one of those few times when we ran before we walked, and it came back to bite us in the ass.

The reality check delivered a clear message: "Stay in your lane, and if you're going to play with the big boys, you have to dot your i's, cross your t's, and get your legal teams out in front of potential issues rather than assum-ing you'll fix them after the fact."

Ultimately, it was a great lesson. We went back to our core, redoubled our efforts to provide education to those who were in need of our products but were on a scale we could manage. By the end of the following year, even with our slow return to full shipping capacity, TriggerPoint grew another 60 percent.

At the end of the day, don't worry about what has hap-pened. Prepare for what is going to happen. Use the bumps in the road as education, use them as leverage, and use them as the platform to make your company great.

WHO AND WHAT DONE WELL: APPLE

Apple is a great example of how all the elements—branding, marketing, product, and sales—come together under the principle of knowing who you are makes you who you want to be.

Steve Jobs knew he was serving the forward-thinking consumer of the future. All he had to do was look at his workforce to know who and what his business was. He created a brand around their values, their emotions, their image of who and what they wanted to be.

The Apple logo says it all. It's simultaneously youthful and nerdy, playing on the association with bringing an apple to your schoolteacher. At the same time, it alludes to the allure of the forbidden—taking a bite out of the apple and suddenly accessing a world of knowledge.

From there, Apple's marketing became an easy matter of pulling their audience to them by capitalizing on those images and emotions. Their advertisements never mention faster processing speed, simple interface, elegant design—all very obvious benefits of their products. Instead, they show images of cool, sexy people living effortless, exciting lives. They evoke the ideal future with an ultrasimple, ultrasexy look and feel.

So when it came to product, Steve Jobs just had to look for the opportunity to disrupt. You could already talk on the phone from anywhere and play music from the palm of your hand. Rather than create a better version of one of these, he put it all into one handheld machine and created the future his branding promised. A future that is now our new normal.

DON'T BE A VICTIM

No matter what it is that you want your company to become, your path to becoming that has to start with a relentless, no-holds-barred reality check about who and what you are today.

You can't massage your own ego as you view the many different variables that threaten your potential for success—from the competitive landscape in your market, to the insecurities hiding within your own head.

As an entrepreneur, you have a choice: to make your path complicated by hiding from your shortcomings or to make it simple by confronting them.

This choice is what makes the difference between spending the next ten years wondering why your business can't seem to rise to the next level or spending those years advocating for your own success by removing the obstacles in your purpose-driven path.

Your mental imprint about your own identity is the vehicle that will drive you to who you want to be in life or your business to be in the world. There is no time to be a victim in the world of entrepreneurship.

If you're ready to stop hiding and start succeeding, take a deep breath and dive headfirst into reality.

CHAPTER 6

A HEALTHY BODY IS A HEALTHY MIND

The body tells the mind to do incredible things, but the mind tells the body to do horrible things.

Our society says, "A healthy mind is a healthy body," meaning that mind-body experiences are what lead to inner peace. You look at yoga, meditation, or other alternative therapies, and they seem to promise that the mind can heal the body.

I call bull on that. It's way more complicated.

If anything, the idea of a mind-body experience is exactly what allows people to sell you things. All they have to do is convince your mind that it's good for you. They don't have to prove anything by its actual effect on your body. If it doesn't have the desired effect on your body, it must just be because your mind isn't strong enough. Buy more, try harder, believe more deeply.

Think back to when we talked about wants versus needs. Your mind is excellent at interpreting a want as a need. It will adapt into any belief system. The mind will allow a want to be interpreted as a need.

> ### PHILIPPIANS 4:19
>
> We can always trust that God will always meet our needs. Whatever we need here on earth he will supply, even if it's to face death, as Paul did. Whatever we need in heaven he will supply. We must remember, however, the difference between our wants and our needs.

However, the mind does this interpretation from a distance. Meanwhile, your gut is always dealing directly with everything that comes at you. It processes everything from the food you eat to the emotions you experience to the beliefs you hold about the world.

GUT VERSUS BRAIN

To me, religion is the same as marketing. Some of the most profitable businesses in the world are religions. Some of the greatest wars in the world have been based off religious views. Religion gives me heartburn, but my relationship with Jesus gives me everything I've ever needed to be comfortable in my own skin.

I had a true need in my life for identity and purpose. When I encountered the Lord, my gut told me it was the right thing for me. I believe that most people know between right and wrong. Their gut confirms that inner knowledge with a physical response about whether a certain action or behavior is good or bad for them.

They may, however, choose to go against it because their brain is overriding their thought process with rationalization about why it's not wrong, why the action is good for them. Over time, their daily life becomes a series of bad choices that build up into a lifetime of stress—all because they took the complicated mental route instead of stripping it down to the simplicity of what their gut already knew.

A lot of thought leaders encourage people in this situation to "think" their way out of the life they've created through their bad choices. If they get their minds right, their bodies will follow. But this is only repurposing the same complicated approach that got those people in trouble to begin with.

Most decisions are quite simple and easy, if we let them

be. They simply require hard actions of us. However, we make them harder by layering confusion on top of everything.

Who's telling me what to do?

What is the right thing?

Where is the path I should follow?

How do I know what I need to do?

I don't know what to do.

I don't know why I'm doing this.

The confusion comes from overthinking. I know so many people who overthought their course of action to the point where they've made themselves sick. They know they shouldn't be doing it, but they're still doing it.

We all know when we've taken a joke too far, pushed the argument too far, or made the wrong choice on something as simple as a shirt, tie, or suit. It's typically doing something to impress others that gets us in trouble. When you make the wrong decision, you have to deal with the fallout.

Your mind typically addresses only symptoms of a problem. But your gut tells you right where the problem lies. When you address the problem, all the symptoms go away. Listening to your gut will simplify your life, correct the bad choices, relieve the stress you've built up over time. From there, it doesn't take your mind long to get on board.

Why do we overthink? Because we haven't accepted who we are in order to become who we want to be in life. We act out a narrative each day without knowing where it came from. We tell ourselves a story about the purpose and meaning of our actions without considering whether that story is accurate and where it might have come from.

Your gut knows all the answers behind who and what you are. Once you get in touch with that inner truth, your body will allow your mind to do things you never thought possible.

So many of the things we try to do for others end up getting in our own way. We say that we're adapting, molding, changing ourselves for the good of our loved ones, our customers, our employees. Meanwhile, our gut is always there, telling us who we're really supposed to be.

It's easier to have an excuse than it is to take the blame. I believe you can take this mindset and apply it to all aspects of your business.

In marketing, for example, if you try too hard, you typically get it wrong. Your gut typically tells you if you've got the right approach. Of course, the mind steps in and overthinks the process, ending up with complexity, missed deadlines, and ultimate confusion, all while the gut is telling you to keep things simple, don't overcomplicate, and talk "to" the customer instead of "at" the customer.

MONEY CAN MAKE YOU BLIND

When you embark on something in life, whether it's starting a company or anything else, it's imperative that you start from a similar sensation of certainty within your gut. If you find yourself overthinking the creation of a product, it might mean that you don't actually believe in your gut that it's the right thing for your customers. If you don't believe that there are people out there in need of your product, you will most likely fail.

On the other hand, when you go into business with the sincere belief that your concept will change the world, as foolish as it may sound to others, you can be sure that you're on the right track.

When you're living your purpose-driven life, the dollars will always be there. More importantly, the internal reward will always be there, no matter how many dollars you have.

I started my business from a place of freedom within my body and mind. With that, I created financial freedom for the rest of my life.

However, as you become more successful, *money can make you blind*. The more money you make, the more tendency there is to override your pure gut instinct. You begin to believe that you ultimately have control over every factor in your success. This belief causes you to overthink every move you make. Instead of leading with positivity and trust, you lead with arrogance and insecurity.

Looking back at all the things I did during my life in Hollywood—being an actor, producing films, starting a production management company—those might have looked like smart moves from the outside. But there was no passion behind what I did.

My gut wasn't telling me to pursue that life. Every action I took came from my mind telling me to do things that allowed me to shelter my ego, fulfill selfish desires, or have new ways to talk about myself—things that soothed the symptoms of my real problem: insecurity.

Yes, I was somewhat successful, but I had to walk away from it all. I didn't know as much then as I do now, but something in me did sense that I was seeking others to define me. My insecurities outweighed my gut-level belief in myself. As hard as I tried to be something better than who and what I was, ultimately, I was left with just me.

Money allows you to cut corners and alienate yourself from the realities of your business.

Money doesn't get you the best employees; passion does. Money allows for high salaries, consultants, and complacency. Don't pay someone to get you out of your problems; instead, take a reality check and deal with your problems yourself.

Listen to your gut, take a reality check, and understand who you are today so you can be exactly who you want to be in the future. Your company depends on it.

CONFIDENCE IS THE DRIVING FORCE TO SUCCESS

With success come insecurities. I really think everyone goes through this. You either go with strong and aggressive or passive and aggressive. Regardless, the outcome is the same: you second-guess who and what you are because all of this second-guessing brings back childhood memories of trying to prove something to someone somewhere. Don't lose your confidence because *confidence is the driving force to success*!

When TriggerPoint reached its period of greatest growth, I realized I needed support. That part was easy. What I didn't share earlier was how much self-doubt came with that realization.

As a result, I allowed others to make me believe that I was fully incapable of being a CEO. People on my executive team told me that because we were making so much money, we needed to put somebody else in my seat—somebody who had a greater education and who was able to manage the business better because of their credentials.

Their words touched on the parts of me that were still raw and vulnerable. Unfortunately, I didn't let my gut guide me through those raw places. I sat in my office and listened to the things my mind told me—that I'm a high school graduate, that I have no degree, that I'm uneducated.

I looked right past all the simple truths I'd learned through street smarts and life experience and focused on the unknown complexity of what they teach in business school.

I wanted to do the best I could for my company, but I also let the money make me stupid. Instead of listening to my gut, I believed all the crap that people were feeding to me. So I brought someone in, knowing in my gut all the while that I shouldn't.

My mind overrode that gut-level knowledge by telling me he was a good friend, that I could trust him to do things the way I'd do them. But as we went through the process of bringing this individual into the team, I started to feel the abrasions of conflict. When we had conflict, we didn't deal with it well. Our conflict created trauma within our own relationship and within my executive team.

This one decision became the greatest challenge of my professional life, all because I ignored my gut and listened to my mind instead.

Overthinking will always distance you from passion. As a result, you'll draw people around you who do not believe in what you believe. These people will pull up every insecurity that you've ever had, not in your best interest but in their own interest. They want you to believe that you need them to achieve financial freedom.

You can't let these people convince you that you're not strong enough, good enough, smart enough. You must follow your gut in hiring people who believe in who and what you are and believe in what you're capable of becoming. You need people around you who know that you're the leader and who want to support you versus wanting to take your seat.

THE BODY OF YOUR BUSINESS

One of my favorite Cassidyisms is this one: *The body tells the mind to do incredible things, but the mind tells the body to do horrible things.*

You'll see this principle play out when circumstances get more stressful than you can handle. I've watched many entrepreneurs get addicted to alcohol, drugs, and harmful behavior because they listen too much to their mind, which keeps insisting they need (or deserve) a crutch to help them deal with their stressful circumstances.

If these entrepreneurs were to listen to their bodies, they would take the rest they need or go out and exercise or reengage with other parts of their life that they've been neglecting. In doing this, they'd find the stress relief they're looking for.

Likewise, your business is a body—one that tries to communicate with you the same way your own body does.

The body of a business is twofold:

- It's the brand identity set by who and what you are as the leader.
- It's the who and what of all the employees in your office.

If your employees are unhealthy in who and what they are, if they are not positive in thought, and if they do not really believe that you're the leader, they will ultimately create cancer within your organization.

If they are selfish about what they're trying to achieve, they won't support what you're trying to achieve. That will become a cancer that slowly deteriorates all the relationships that make up the body of your business.

So how can you avoid that?

First, by following your gut in who you hire. Second, in how you contribute to the health of your business body through caring for your employees on a personal level.

A great parallel is found in the old adage, "You are what you eat." The food you consume ultimately defines who you are. If you eat crap every day, you will feel like crap every day. In the same way, if you treat your employees like crap every day, they will treat you like crap every day. What you bring into that office is the nutritional value that your employees feed upon.

This is why your communication skill is so important. Your mouth is the door to your office. Every day that you open it, you've got to lead your workplace in being healthy. You must bring positivity into that office so that everybody feels great about who and what they are.

I'll be honest—I was not always great at that. I often came into work thinking, *I paid all you guys to be my friends. You guys need to be nice to me and appreciate all that I'm giving you.*

What a screwed-up way to look at it.

I'd never feed my body garbage and then get mad at it for not performing at the level I expect. It's the same thing if I treat my employees like crap but expect them to still give me their A game back.

The truth was that I always loved my employees in my heart. And by the time I exited TriggerPoint, I was very appreciative of all my employees and felt they did a fantastic job for me. Unfortunately, not all of them knew how much I cared about them.

Because I carried the weight of the world into that office every day, I communicated that stress to my employees without even knowing I was doing it.

THE WEIGHT OF LIFE

Each responsibility or pressure that comes into your life first enters through your mind. As you grow, your mind becomes filled with relationships, making a living, bills, traffic, weather, world events. Eventually, it gets so full that you can't carry it in your head, so you transfer the weight somewhere else.

For most people, it gets transferred to their upper back. There's a reason why everyone gets tension in their neck and shoulders and can never resist a shoulder massage when it's offered. You're essentially wearing a spiritual backpack stuffed with the pressures that your mind can't deal with. There's a common metaphor for this. We call it "baggage."

If you look around, you can literally see this baggage weighing people down. The middle-aged businessman has a hunch in his neck. The little old lady who has lived through wars, a fifty-year marriage, and parenting multiple kids is bent almost double over her walker. By contrast, children stand completely straight. The weight of life isn't a thing yet for them.

Some people think the answer to the weight of life is to lessen the load. You may want to eliminate pressures by living a more "minimal" lifestyle, but that might not be a real solution as far as the happiness of your spouse or kids.

So what can you do about the weight of life?

When you're a founder, pressure is inevitable. Some try to shoulder it alone. Others lean heavily on their employees. Either way is detrimental to the whole-body health of your organization, because whoever bears the bulk of this weight thinks they have a right to be a turd.

You can only counter the weight of life by creating integrity at the most basic levels. If you're physically out of shape—meaning your company isn't prepared to handle the stress of normal operations—you're creating a situation where you will work yourself to death.

Before long, you'll be doing the same thing to your employees. If you're refusing to apply discipline and create balance in your life that lets you handle the pressures well, those pressures will weigh more heavily on you. Before long, you'll toss those pressures onto the backs of your employees, causing stress and injury.

However, if you take care of yourself and invest in your employees' well-being the same way that you invest in your own, your staff will love you. They will naturally gravitate toward helping you shoulder the weight of those pressures.

Nobody will be working any harder than any other

person. Everyone will function optimally the way they are designed to. The body of your business will develop integrity that lets you move forward with greater speed and efficiency.

When you address the problem at its most basic level, all the symptoms go away. You've got a great staff. You've got a great business. You've got a great way of life.

THE INJURY CYCLE

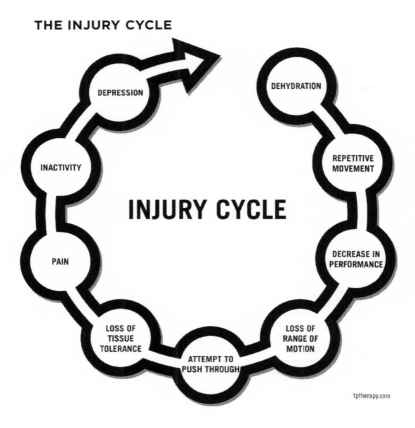

When you're first starting out, you have no idea how vulnerable entrepreneurship can make you. Your passion makes you feel invincible until your idea becomes a reality.

However, once you have a product that you want to put in customers' hands, you suddenly feel a whole new level of vulnerability. You have a product you want people to buy. You have a brand you want your employees to live. You might have a family that you want to support or loans you want to pay off. At the very least, you want appreciation for all the hard work you've put in, trying to do good in the world.

That's the same thing that your employees want. They feel the way you treat them and think, *I don't want fancy perks or a corner office. I just want somebody to appreciate me.*

The mind tells you to do more, to try harder, to be something you're not in order to get the appreciation you desire. You'll start overthinking everything. But when you strip away the complexity, your gut instinct will give the simplest answer possible: to have a healthy mind, you need to have a healthy body.

Having a healthy body is very simple: avoid injury.

The injury cycle is something most performance athletes are familiar with. It tracks with the biorhythms of your body so closely that you could almost set your watch by it. So let's use the clock as a guide for understanding this cycle—first as an athlete, then as an entrepreneur.

THE ATHLETE'S VIEW

Let's say you start training at 12:00 p.m.—hands at the top of the clock. You've already gotten through your morning routines. You've fueled your body. You've warmed up. You're ready to put in the hard yards.

By one o'clock, you've hit your stride. With each minute that passes, you're getting faster, stronger, more functional and focused. You're in the zone, and it feels amazing.

But then at three o'clock, that trajectory changes. Your muscles are getting fatigued. Your focus is beginning to lag. But you don't want to give up. You're hungry for those gains. You don't want to lose that amazing flow. So you decide to push through.

As the clock progresses—from four to five and on to six— you're feeling the change hard. You start to feel the lack of tissue tolerance. You can tell that you're getting dehydrated, and you know you should stop. But you want to end on a high note. Your performance is starting to suffer, but you don't want to stop until you at least get back to the same level at which you started six hours ago.

So you keep on.

By nine o'clock, you've done everything that you can to get through that process. You've pushed so hard that you start to break. But when you start to break, you don't know anything other than to continue to push. You're doing this, forgetting what you already know: that once you've pushed yourself past your limit, to where your body cannot tolerate the demand you're placing on it, a compromise will occur. It's not a matter of how. It's a matter of when.

By 11:00 p.m., you're done. You've injured yourself. You've gone from premium performance to a near-complete lack of ability to move. By the time you limp home, you're deep in what we call athletic-induced depression—the dark cloud that looms over your life when you can no longer do what you love to do.

THE ENTREPRENEUR'S VIEW

The injury cycle relates to the entrepreneur's day in much the same ways it does for an athlete.

By 12:00 p.m., you've gotten through your morning

routines. You've answered your emails, done your staff meetings, fueled the fire for the flames of your success. You're amped and ready to get in the zone and get crap done.

By one or two o'clock, you're really hitting your stride. You're experiencing those gains of understanding who and what you are. Data is coming together; strategies are being formed.

But by three o'clock, you begin to feel some resistance. Instinctively, you push back. You push yourself, you push your employees, and you push your vendors. Pushing against the resistance you feel creates an abrasion—slight at first, but it grows as the day goes on.

This is when you start to get dehydrated. Decisions are foggy; coffee becomes the go-to.

Your mind begins telling you that your feeling of power and purpose earlier in the day is slipping through your fingers. You begin to overthink: *Am I good enough? Am I strong enough? Do people like me? Am I the only one who's working hard around here?*

Rather than addressing the root problem of that abrasion, you ignore it. You decide to push through. More coffee, more stimulants, more reliance on yourself than on others.

When your employees approach you, you shut down and fail to communicate thoroughly. When your partners ask if everything's OK, you give a one-word answer.

Communication equals hydration for the body of business. Without it, your workplace functionality begins to really suffer.

By four and five o'clock, you start to really get frustrated. You don't want to leave without getting back some of the great feeling you had at 12:00 p.m., so you call home and say you'll be working late. This leads to abrasion within your personal life, which creates further dehydration through lack of communication.

The feeling of pushing through should be your cue for an instant reality check. Your gut is stepping in to tell you there's something you need to stop, look, and listen to. Unfortunately, what most entrepreneurs do is isolate themselves from their team. *If they don't support me the way I need, I'll win this on my own.*

By the time 6:00 p.m. rolls around, people start looking at each other, wondering whether it's OK to leave or not. They can see things aren't OK, but you haven't communicated your expectations, so they don't know what else to do.

Somewhere between 6:00 p.m. and 9:00 p.m., you

become the "eleventh-hour" guy. You charge into a room and flip out on everybody. Nobody's implemented the sales strategy correctly, nobody's met the marketing objective, nobody's made progress on the goal. You have to redo everything yourself, because apparently, you're the only one who cares about this company.

It doesn't take long after everyone leaves for you to realize what you've done: you've injured the relationships and, with them, your business functionality. By 12:00 a.m., depression sets in. For entrepreneurs, this usually means drinking, smoking, doing whatever they can to hide from the fact that they failed at doing what they love.

The fact that most entrepreneurs go to bed thinking about what they did wrong, not what they did right, indicates that they don't understand or aren't respecting the "injury cycle" of their business. They aren't doing the small things to build a healthy business body, and as a result, their minds are plagued by worry, frustration, and insecurity.

BREAKING THE INJURY CYCLE

One of the hardest things for people to understand is that they *can* break the injury cycle. Between each hour on the clock, there is an opportunity for you to take care of yourself, to correct the demons in your mind that are causing a lack of health in your body. It's very simple, but you have to be aware of who and what you are to be able to do that.

Just as every day has twenty-four hours, every activity in your life has this cycle. If you just keep a clock in mind in every relationship or situation, you know when the peak performance hours will be and when you start feeling the resistances that make you want to push through. By knowing this, you can prevent those injuries from taking place.

The simplest way to do this is to eliminate yourself from the equation and do something that hydrates your spirit.

INDEPENDENT YET AS ONE

The human body is built for each muscle to act independently yet as one. The body of your business is built the same way.

Ironically, the Bible uses that same analogy for how believers are supposed to function. It calls us the "body of Christ," and tells us to act independently yet as one. Personally, I use my relationship with Christ to be that buffer between mind and body. It gives me an awareness of myself. It reassures me of my intrinsic value, which allows me to accept who and what I am.

It's essential to find at least one thing in your life that

grounds you. For me, it's the relationship with Christ, but for others, it's a relationship with their spouse, their parents, or their siblings. For others still, it's their relationship to a specific place or activity—a spot overlooking the ocean, a park where they take their kids to play, a quiet room in their house where they can still their thoughts and just breathe.

Just as you always need a great assistant to support you where you're weak, you always need someone or something to ground you in reality. These are the relationships that help you see the space between the moment of peak performance and the moment when it's time to pull back. These are the forces that pull your focus off what your mind is telling you so that you can be informed by what your body is intuiting from the world around you.

If there's one thing that I hope this book does for you, it's to find that grounding force in your own life.

As a leader, you cannot lead by force. The weight of life and the injury cycle come about through a pursuit of an individual win. Entrepreneurs often don't know any other way to be; they think as individuals, they dream in terms of individual success. But if you want your company to win in the marketplace, that win has to be collective. You must create a collaboration within your team that lets you win individually yet as one.

Leadership in a company is not a dictatorship. I don't mean this as a moral imperative; I mean that it simply doesn't work that way. Founders' common belief that their individual efforts define their company's success is the precise reason why so few small businesses succeed.

You *can't* do everything in your business, at least not at the level it needs to be done. You can't be everything to everyone. The reason company dictatorship never works is because your employees know that you need them. If you want to get the best performance out of them, you also must acknowledge how much you need them.

The only reason your company has gone as far as it has is because there was collaboration every day along the way. You may have ignored those collaborations because you were moving so fast, but they have brought you to where you are today and will ultimately define your success in the future.

Everyone has a purpose, everyone has a place on the team, and everyone should be appreciated for their efforts. All should work independently yet as one for the greater good of the company!

CHAPTER 7

TOO MUCH MONEY
MAKES YOU STUPID

I lived through the dot-com era of the late 1990s and early 2000s, when every internet company was overvalued. One day, a reality check came, and the stock market said, "This is a bunch of BS. Not all of these companies are worth as much as they seem to be."

In May 2000, that bubble burst, and a lot of people's lifestyles burst with it.

Now, almost twenty years later, we seem to be reentering that era. Snapchat just debuted with the largest IPO ever. And what is Snapchat exactly? Just temporary information and pictures, designed for entertainment.

That's the Holy Grail that all these new entrepreneurs are seeking: not something that lasts but something simple, even simplistic, that will let them create a big enough splash to sell high and get out.

These young entrepreneurs have burned through a lot of venture capitalist money to get there. Once they got the money, though, they became stupid.

By contrast, you can look back at Steve Jobs. He didn't have any money, but he and Steve Wozniak built a computer that was better than any other computer in the world. How did they do it?

They identified a need, and they created a product to facilitate that need. What they built has resonated deeply ever since. From that day on, Apple's inventions—not just the products but the brand around it—have been duplicated in various ways by other companies aspiring to the same kind of greatness.

These days, everybody wants to create a start-up, not realizing that starting a business means potentially disrupting an industry. As soon as they encounter the problems that stem from disruption, they set about raising a lot of capital to be able to take care of the problems.

But money doesn't take care of the problems.

The problems have to do with everything else we've talked about in this book. The problems have to do with you as a person and the way you run and lead your organization. In fact, the less money you have, the more quickly you can identify the problems because you have to work harder to solve them.

Working harder makes money actually mean something. When your business gets to the point where you have money, you're then able to communicate about it in a way that makes sense. Communication is what allows you to facilitate the right person in accurately addressing that problem.

Those who have too much money from the very beginning don't have a clue about how to run a business. They feel like they can go hire the right equation, they can throw money at problems, and they can use money to be the vehicle for reason. That is why the statistics are so high on so many companies failing.

Just take a minute and Google how many start-ups fail in the first year. It's crazy. Times have changed as well. Look at how many companies five years old or younger haven't made a profit. The young guys of today are professional money raisers, while, at the same time, company failures.

There's an old saying that "necessity is the mother of

invention." That idea defines sustainable success. Money tends to foster complex, sophisticated plans (or, honestly, the lack thereof), but plans like that tend to get in the way of fulfilling a simple need.

You overevaluate a situation to the point where you don't clearly see how to bring it to fruition. You end up trying to hire all these different people to solve the problems, without even knowing what the problems are.

I want to be as clear as I can be here: money has no feeling, no personality, and no rational decision-making ability.

Yet, when a human has it, they feel powerful, entitled, and able to conquer anything because people love and "respect" other people with money. If you truly don't know how to manage your money, the chances are good that you are going to run out of it. How many people have won the lottery and lost their life because they don't know how to manage their money?

I really believe that there are CEOs in this world who have raised a bunch of money and don't know what to do with it, so they start throwing it at employees, parties, and fabricated problems. They end up living out of the company, hiding from the reality that their burn is greater than their income.

BUILDING YOUR BRAND WITH NO CASH

Let me remind you that I had no real money when I started TriggerPoint, so I had to rely on my resources and relationships rather than money. Here are some tips for building your brand with no cash.

1. Use all the marketable relationships you can to build your brand. Ask friends and family to support your brand verbally and on social media, and carry fliers around to hand out to people who might be interested in your products.

2. If you can build your business on the backs of others, then that's fantastic. Build business relationships with people who don't compete with one another and instead support one another unconditionally. Don't focus on the dollars; focus on the support you give one another.

3. This is a tough one: if you can piggyback your company on the back of your current employer, you'll give yourself a better chance of surviving. This is really tough because you have to burn the candle on both ends, and if your employer sees you taking time and resources from your paying job, you'll probably be fired. If they know about what you're doing, you never know, they may support the venture if your current company doesn't see you as competition.

4. Spend money on manufacturing, find any marketable opportunity, and trade your time or expertise rather than having to pay in cold hard cash.

5. Try to use a credit card where you get miles so that every dollar you spend has twice the value. Hotels, cars, and flights can all be paid for in miles. Ask friends and family if you can have their miles if they are not using them. Miles are very valuable to a start-up.

6. Slow growth is fine because you can afford it. Grow too fast and you might not have the money to keep growing.

A real entrepreneur doesn't need money. If you have a clear need and a will to fulfill it, you'll just do it. It may be rudimentary and ugly, like my Frankenball was in the beginning, but you'll get to where you need to go if you focus on your vision and are smart with your money.

In the end, they fail, all because they started the company with too much money.

I have the greatest respect for all the bootstrappers out there who have become multimillionaires with passion and a shoestring budget. They didn't create their empires because they had money behind them; they did it because there was an integral need in society for whatever they created.

Your first product doesn't have to be sophisticated. It just has to exist.

Once it exists, you have a proof of concept, which you then validate by using the rudimentary product to fulfill the need on as many test customers as you can find. That's when you can go out and get the money you need to refine your product into something sophisticated.

Few young entrepreneurs consider what it means to take a VC's money before they do it. They find out quickly how much heartache, strain, and stress are created by someone standing over you, waiting for their investment to pay off. As we've already learned, stress breaks things—relationships, first and foremost. And as we've also learned, relationships are the fibrous bands that make up a business.

Lack of money, on the other hand, doesn't create stress;

it creates pressure. You think incessantly about how you can get it done. But you don't have an expectation or a time constraint. It's simply the weight of your passion creating that pressure.

Pressure is something that actually keeps people together. The more pressure, the more opportunity for an explosion.

Of course, the explosion can be good or bad, but when all those who are involved are working together, it's amazing how they come together with clear communication and a healthy dose of pressure.

EMOTIONAL VALUE VERSUS DOLLAR VALUE

Have you ever noticed that people who feel like they don't need much money always seem happy? It pisses me off sometimes, but it's true. Whenever you're considering money, it's always a question of what you need. Do you need more things? Or do you need the right things for you?

This is an essential question when you're building a business. At the very beginning, a great litmus test for the new employees you're hiring is to be frank with them about your money situation.

You can tell an employee, "I do not have any money today,

but there is an equity in this potentially for you. This is all I have to pay you today, but I hope to pay you more tomorrow." This changes the conversation completely. Some people will walk out, making your decision easy. But others will connect to your passion and your company's purpose.

The people you want working for you more than anyone else are the ones who choose themselves for you. If your new hire comes into your business thinking about how they can do good in the world, they will translate those opportunities into dollars.

Contrast that with hiring from an abundance of money. You can overpay for somebody, thinking that they can do the right job without ever even having a conversation about the raw realities of the business. Without realizing it, you assume that the amount of money you're paying them means they can and should be able to read your mind.

But just as no amount of money can create a need in your market, no amount of money can create passion or purpose in your employee.

I started TriggerPoint with no money of my own—just a $17,000 loan from my grandmother. But I was flush with passion and emotional payoff because I knew without question that I was living my purpose-driven life.

The way I was living looked like hand to mouth in the beginning, but for me, the experience was euphoric. I didn't even realize we were profitable until we'd grown so much that we needed an office, a supply chain, a more cost-effective means of production to fulfill our orders efficiently.

However, the positivity around profitability turned a corner at a certain point. When we passed the mark of $10 million in sales, the whole business changed. At that point, I realized the emotional connection I had with the end consumer had deteriorated.

No longer was I standing in a booth, telling people how they could enhance their health and lifestyle through implementing the strategies around the product; instead, I was on a video, trying to convey that same message through a screen instead of a one-on-one connection. You could still see the passion in me. I would put everything I had into the videos. People loved the education, inspiration, and motivation. I was still feeding their needs, but I wasn't feeding mine.

I was doing fewer speaking engagements, but I was teaching the methodologies less. The personal interactions were diminishing; instead, it became all about numbers, closed-door meetings, hiring, firing, margins, accounts receivable, and payables. I was flying around the world, not to teach and interact with those who were in need, but rather, setting up distribution and intense negotiations.

I realized that my passion was on the back burner because I no longer had that emotional transaction with the people who made me feel like I had a purpose, like I was making the world a better place.

I had actually transferred my emotional dollars into a codependency with the physical dollar. For a time, the integrity behind the brand was lost because we were focused more on money than we were on changing people's lives.

THE REWARDS OF FAMILY

Family is family, for better or for worse. You don't always get the loving, nurturing experience you want, but you learn how to deal with those with whom you have conflict because they're the only family you will ever have.

When you're all together for holidays, such as Thanksgiving and Christmas, even though there might be dysfunction throughout the year, you can't help but feel the reward of putting in the work together to strengthen your unbreakable bond. The unconditional love that we celebrate in families is defined by the hard work of getting through those conflicts.

As an entrepreneur, you spend just as much time with your company as you do with your family (sometimes even more). You have to be willing to learn how to get through those conflicts. You have to create that unconditional love within your company if you want to reap the rewards you seek.

Money is great. Expanding feels awesome. But there is nothing like the feeling of coming together over a common goal and celebrating together once you've reached it. The validation in that moment outweighs any financial gain your company might make.

One of the greatest experiences that I had at TriggerPoint was when I brought my wife back into the business. It was thirteen years after we started the company as a couple with an Airstream trailer and a dream. We put a slideshow together with photos from those beginning years and showed it to the entire company.

This really exposed our employees to the passion that she and I had for the brand in the very beginning. It showed how our passion had grown from our team of just two into a workforce of forty-nine people in the office, with many more connected as distributors, manufacturers, sales reps, and the list goes on.

For us, it reaffirmed that no matter how hard we worked

in the beginning and how many conflicts we had along the way, it was totally worth it. We were deploying capital to families, children, and future entrepreneurs.

TriggerPoint wasn't a network of forty-nine individuals but forty-nine families.

When we got home that night, my wife and I compared notes and realized we'd been feeling the same thing: it was like we had forty-nine children whom we were helping to raise. Like any parents, we just hoped that we could get it done the right way.

Then we looked at our young kids, and I said, "I hope we can do it the right way for them too." There is no textbook for leadership, as a parent or as a CEO. All you can do is do your best, lead with love, and care about all those who are in need of your brand. If you do that, you will be successful. Without that, you're on a path of anxiety, frustration, and lack of focus because you forgot why you started in the first place.

At the end of the day, the emotional currency that you carry in life is much more valuable than the hard currency.

Giving a smile to one of your hardworking employees in the right moment is worth more than if you gave them a hundred bucks. The hard yards are won by the small choices—to be vulnerable, to place the emotional value over the dollar, to invest your time and resources in what means the most.

> **MATTHEW 5:16**
>
> You should be a light for other people. Live so that they will see the good things you do and praise your Father in heaven.

When you lead with that emotional connection, most employees won't know what to do with it. It motivates them to put out a performance that makes more money than you know what to do with. It's that simple.

CHAPTER 8

PASSION BEFORE PROCESS

You could look at the things I did before I started Trigger-Point and see success.

I started my own production management company in Los Angeles, I competed at an elite level in some of the most demanding sports that exist, and I managed to get through school despite being hampered by serious learning disabilities.

Despite the money I made, the number of powerful people I connected with, or the acclaim I received, I look back at those phases of my life and see failure—not in the activities themselves but in what was driving them.

True, I had some fun and learned a lot along the way. But in the final call, those phases of my life were failure because there was misguided passion behind them.

My passion was more for pride, fame, accolades than it was for my true heart. My purpose-driven life is to serve others, not to serve myself. Most of my life prior to TriggerPoint was totally more about me than it was about others.

When I founded TriggerPoint, my true passion was revealed. It allowed me to look back and see everything in my past with crystal clarity. As much as I loved the activities that had defined my previous life—athletics, acting, entrepreneurship—they all broke down into ego-centric self-promotion. As a result, they broke me down too, physically and emotionally.

But with TriggerPoint, I'd found something that allowed me to channel my skills, talents, and knowledge into passionate advocacy for others.

TriggerPoint also gave clarity and shape to my early life. When I was a kid, people used to predict that I'd be an actor. But when I shut my eyes and thought about what I wanted to be when I grew up, I remember wanting to become some kind of physical therapist as well as an athlete. Ironically, once I really found my passion in life, it actually mirrored those two things in a very practical manner.

I had forgotten all about those childhood dreams because I'd been doing everything I loved in the wrong way, trying to live my life within the bounds of what others told me was possible.

It was an amazing revelation in my early thirties to find myself living out my childhood dream, just in a way I never knew was possible. It was even more amazing to realize that being true to myself and my own passion, I could do the most good in helping others.

In the end, in order to find my true success, my financial freedom, my ability to be who I'm supposed to be in life, I had to be stripped down and built back up. Once I was built back up, it was clear to me that all the years that I put the attention on myself was for trying to fill a hole that could never be filled in the first place.

FINDING FLOW

Most passionate people are very emotional people as well. They don't live in a black-and-white world; they live in a gray world. That grayness not only tarnishes their accomplishments, but it also alienates them from everything objective.

When you let your emotions get the better of you, you not only obsess over the pluses and minuses in a given day, but you also absorb them all. You typically forget the positives, and you obsess only about the negatives.

I can remember standing in a booth at health fairs, trying to prove to people that they needed our products. After we packed up, I'd spend the rest of my waking hours obsessing about the one or two people who didn't feel the benefit of our products or who challenged our professional credibility instead of concentrating on the ninety-eight people who left feeling empowered and hopeful.

Passion thrives on flow. When it encounters roadblocks, it trends toward obsession. If you don't discipline this obsession into a productive channel, it will end up turning on you. You can eat up all your energy by trying to answer the question, "How can I convert these customers into believing in what I'm doing and why I'm doing it?"

The answer is that there's no answer.

That was a big learning process for me because I didn't know how to look between a goal and a dream.

A goal is obtainable because it has a concrete outcome, one that you can measure, touch, and experience in real life. But a dream is there only while your eyes are shut. When you open them, it's gone.

Some people pursue their passion by constantly building bigger dreams. Others pursue their passion by setting their minds to accomplish goals. It's the difference between standing on the beach and contemplating the horizon of the ocean, and standing on a football field staring down the end zone. One is conceptual; the other is concrete.

It may seem like a small difference, but it makes a big difference in terms of how you treat the people closest to you.

When you're chasing a dream, it's natural to ignore the people who want to measure, build processes, and provide discipline. Instead, you embrace the people who give you accolades, who tell you to keep dreaming, that you're amazing for having such lofty visions of the future.

But when you're in pursuit of a goal, you marshal the people around you who can help you get there. You crave accountability and support. You embrace discipline and process from those who provide it, knowing that it will build guardrails around your passion that allow you to go full bore without worrying about getting off track.

Every person who is in your life as an entrepreneur is

there for a reason. At the end of the day, if you're truly passionate about what you're doing, you should see all of those people as a benefit.

Remember, you're not a child anymore. You don't need to prove your independence to anybody. The people in your organization who question and challenge you are doing it to support you, not to tear you down. You need to reward them and support them in questioning you because they are the ones who will take your business to the next level.

DON'T LET YOUR PASSION GET LOST IN TRANSLATION

Earlier, we talked about the importance of understanding who and what your business is in order for it to be who and what you want it to be. That principle is critical for your business as you figure out how to make passion and process work together.

As we've already said, your business needs people who have passion to help fuel the fire of your brand. But within that passionate pool, you need more than people who express their passion the same way you do—through ideas, emotions, and vision.

You also need people who are oriented toward expressing their passion through process. As a company leader, your success lies in attracting both types of people into your workforce and then learning to manage and motivate both types to work in balance with each other.

Like most entrepreneurs, my nature is extremely passionate about what I do. I'm driven by the emotional connection that I have with the end consumers. This means I can sit in a room and talk until the people around me are deaf, dumb, and blind about how I plan to change the world.

It may set the vision, it may feed everyone else's passion, but if I don't have someone in the room who is strong on the process side of things, nothing I said is likely to happen. It will fade out because there's no documented communication that will guide and inform people going forward.

Sales and marketing are the direct arms of passion, while operations and supply chain are direct arms of process. You have to allow operations to put processes into your strategy so that they can actually get pulled off.

However, these two departments speak two different languages. Operations people see the world in ones and twos, while sales/marketing people speak in poetry. Even when they want the same ultimate goal, they will find reasons to battle against each other.

As a leader, you have to frequently bring both teams back to the common goal, helping them see how to use their strengths to support each other's objectives.

Bear in mind, these battles don't happen until you're at least five years into your company's life span. This is the bare minimum it takes to build a substantial business. Within that first five-year period, you're running almost purely on the fumes of passion. You're all about getting the sales that allow you to grow.

But at year five, you have to start really thinking about building process into the equation—essentially, looking back and figuring out how to do what you've been doing. If you don't create a good process-oriented plan of how you got to where you are, it's going to be very confusing to duplicate what you've done.

Additionally, creating this plan is also a great way to communicate the differences between the way that old and new employees work together.

Many companies never take that look back to think about replicable models for their success. They don't think about the importance of process-oriented people until they've outrun their own capacity, losing customers because they can't keep up with demand or retention.

Nobody likes change, and building a value for process into your passion-oriented culture is incredibly difficult. Even when you're asking employees to do the same things, simply in a different (process-oriented) way, they tend to balk against it.

As the leader, it's on you to relieve the stress. As usual, you do this by hydrating the body of your business with—you guessed it—communication.

"Listen, we're implementing a process today that will allow seamlessness for the future. We're not doing it to change who you are. We're doing it to change how we get the outcome. Because going forward, the outcomes get bigger and more strategic. With bigger plans, there are more people involved. Everyone needs to know their position so that the team can pull it off."

Communication is critical because everyone is relying on you to tell them where they should be. Be clear, simple, and to the point, and all should execute well. Staying with the fifty-thousand-foot view, speaking in generalities, and allowing them to figure it out on their own will create dysfunction and confusion.

Your communication to the team sets the tone for communication between your departments. And in order to effectively communicate, you have to change your communication style by department.

HIRING AN ASSISTANT IS MORE THAN A LUXURY

A great assistant pays for themselves. In many cases, the most passionate entrepreneurs I know look at this as a luxury. And yes, when you're still proving your concept, trying to make money, living out of the back of your car, an assistant is the last thing on your list of must-haves.

But once you're making money, even if you can't pay yourself because you're paying employees to get product into your customers' hands, a great assistant should become a top-of-list priority.

The reason is simple: you need someone to lean on. The bigger you grow, the less freedom you have to bring everything home to your spouse. No one really cares how hard you're working. If you can double up your work capacity, great.

You've got no excuses—if you're not taking care of yourself, your dependents, your employees, it's your fault. An assistant can handle the nuts and bolts, sorting the paper and plastic while you're getting the big stuff done.

Like everyone else in your company, your assistant needs to be someone who really believes in your passion but also understands you as a person. They need to be able to serve as your translator to everyone else in the company so that the emotions that attend your passion don't turn into stress that breaks down the fiber holding everyone together.

This kind of assistant is extremely hard to find. So the last thing you want to do when you find them is underpay and underappreciate them.

Early on, I burned through assistants like I burn through running shoes because I didn't know how to work with them. I expected them to read my mind, forgetting that they were newly minted college graduates with student loans to pay off on the low salary I had to offer them.

They were really nice people, but I relied on them for expertise that they didn't have. They'd walk in and I'd say, "Oh great, you're here. Here's a huge file of stuff for you to do. By the way, go through all my emails and write me an update every day on what emails I need to reply to and what meetings I may have missed today. While you're doing that, gather all the notes from all the other managers or executives, and put them into my phone so that I can read up and know exactly what they've done."

You've got to be pretty damned experienced to be able to do all that on day one.

At that point, I began hiring assistants very differently. I knew I was putting my baby in their hands, so to speak. When I made the choice to hire them, I said, "Listen, you're going to have more leverage over this company than anyone else. It's yours to use, or it's yours to abuse. Whichever one, you will have that opportunity, and you will know when it happens. I hope you use it for the right reasons, not the wrong reasons."

Not all of them believed me when I said this. Those who did now have very high-level jobs at the company. They're still moving the needle for TriggerPoint. I believe that's because I exposed them to the right things, relied on them to execute, and they learned along the way.

If you hire someone to help you, let them help you. With an assistant, you're paying them to get back some of your time in the day. As a busy entrepreneur, buying back your time with an assistant can be one of the best investments you make.

BEING VULNERABLY STRATEGIC

Leaders believe that they can do anything, no matter what. Whether they have a team of one or twenty or two thousand, they persist in believing that they can do everything single-handedly, purely by dint of their passion. Their passion is so strong that they can't conceive of any limitation in their ability to achieve it.

But as we've said, passion usually comes hand in hand with emotion, and emotion has a way of making passion a lot more difficult to translate.

As a leader, you want to lead with every emotion possible. However, being emotionally open is a vulnerable way to live, let alone a vulnerable way to lead. You need to be able to express your passion authentically without letting it affect your employees' morale.

In the end, all you're trying to do is hold on to this rocket ship that you've created out of passion and wrap your head around how you're getting where you're going. That's one of the Achilles' heels of a successful entrepreneur if they start trying to keep up with everybody and not trusting anybody. This creates a huge conflict.

You hire people because you trust them, and that's it. You can't let your brain make the decision based on their education, credentials, or even their experience in the industry. Your gut will tell you the moment you have your first meeting with them whether or not they're the right person for the position.

In my career—before TriggerPoint as well as in it—I hired as a way of filling a void in my life. Much like looking for a doctor to "fix" my broken-down body, I was always looking for someone to take care of the things in my business that I didn't want to put time into understanding. It wasn't until much later in my career that I began trusting my gut to help me hire the right person.

In the beginning, most people, brands, and companies are trying to be all things to everybody. But by allowing your passion to completely guide you, it's easy to get derailed by chasing what turn out to be "shiny objects"—things that promise quick success but have no real opportunity attached to them.

It's essential that you pull away from your passion at times so that you can put more process in to support the body of your company.

Think about your own body and all the processes that support your passion. Your skin is composed of fibers and nerves. Your bones offer structural integrity so that your muscles can act independently yet as one. Your heartbeat is an amazing electrical process that distributes blood throughout your body.

Your blood is what carries the nutrients that give you the freedom, energy, and ability to be who it is that you're supposed to be, whether it be you as a person or you as a business. Without those processes, not only do you not move forward, but you also don't live for very long.

Everything that makes your business meaningful has a process behind it. Learning these processes may seem like a waste of your time, but knowing what they do is crucial to making sure your passion can run unfettered. In order for you to pull off your dream, you have to translate it into goals.

In order to fulfill those goals, you've got to put people under you who believe in who and what you are, who will create the processes that allow you to channel your passion. You have to build your core up with knowledge and information that will inform those who are the extremities, out there in the world, making others believe in your company's cause.

Think of a marathon runner. If you're hard-headed enough on your first marathon, you can do the least amount of training and still get past the finish line. It's like beginners' luck: "I don't know how I finished the race. It just happened."

Then run the race the same way—with minimal training—and see if you get the same result.

Most of the time, when someone is asked to repeat a task the same way they did before, they can't. Why?

Because they didn't follow a process.

They never wrote anything down. They just executed. In the business world, there are way too many dangers to just wing it. Maybe you can in the beginning, but as you grow, you need to get your processes in place so that you can run faster than ever, know when and how things get done, and make everything replicable. That way, new and old employees alike can let their passions run free within your processes.

CHAPTER 9

FIRST INNOVATION AND EDUCATION, THEN PRODUCT

Innovation begins where everyone else stops.

What does this mean to you? *Innovation begins where everyone else stops.*

The innovations of today are so incredibly cool because they go beyond your typical thought process. Most companies start with a product and end with a marketing plan. There is nothing new about this process, other than perhaps the product.

But come on, don't we have enough products in the world

with no real purpose? You use it once and *boom!* it goes into a closet or a drawer.

A true innovation supports the *needs* of your customers.

Most companies come up with a genius product, build a marketing strategy around it, and then go out to find people to buy it.

I built TriggerPoint through the opposite principle. My innovation started not with my product but with my approach to the market. My desire to empower others and do good in the world was the first innovative element in my business.

Once I had the product, that innovative way of seeing the market led me to build my business through education, not through slick traditional methods of marketing. Only at the end of that chain did we introduce the customer to the product.

Ask yourself, are you trying to change the world, or are you trying to take advantage of the world?

Innovators change the world; everybody else takes advantage of the world. If you're not innovating, don't make a product that you think can change the world, because it won't. Innovation is really the key to making your mark in an industry.

You either lead the change and thrive, or you take advantage of the true drivers in the market, making you a me-too product. There is nothing wrong with this. You just have to know that is what you are.

I am a big believer in market disruption or, as I like to say it, punching a hole in a market that otherwise wouldn't exist. This is where the real fun is for a true entrepreneur.

One of the best examples of this is Zappos. Their approach really changed the way people look at business and how to run it. Zappos allowed their people to be unique individuals within their businesses. For all the people stuck in an old-school mentality, it was crazy. It was the kind of thing that kills a company, according to conventional wisdom. You can't give people freedom to be who they want to be within an office.

Lo and behold, they didn't just keep the company alive, but they built it into one of the leading online brands and redefined the nature of employment. People literally tour their headquarters just to get a feel for this revolutionary office environment.

When it comes to sales and marketing strategies, innovation is what separates you from everybody else. As I've said before, I truly believe that education is marketing with integrity. If you want to really create brand loyalty, you have to educate your customer not only about what the product is and what it does but also on how that product can change their life over the long haul.

How are you planning to impact their world? How are you empowering them to be who they want to be in life?

As usual, one of the best examples of this is Apple. When Steve Jobs decided to innovate within his industry, he started by educating customers on why they needed technological innovation in their lives. Only then did he show them the product. In 1994, not everybody had an MP3 player. It was a luxury item until Steve Jobs brought out the iPod and made it a necessity. Not only could you upload music files, but you could also pack it with audio books, podcasts, and even courses through iPod University.

As for the music, no longer did you have to upload your music library file by file. Instead, you could sync it automatically from your computer. And if you suddenly heard a song and wanted it, you could instantly purchase, download, and add it to your library. All of this in a tiny machine that you could carry around in your pocket. Suddenly, it wasn't a luxury item. It was a necessity.

Then Steve Jobs decided to take it one step further: he put the entire thing into a phone. Everybody thought that

that was crazy back in the day. It was something nobody had ever done before. There was a lot of education that had to go into how to use it. It was innovative. It was cool.

Where Steve Jobs applied the most innovation, however, was in making technology sexy. Most electronics at that time were made out of plastic. Apple broke away from that model and started offering their products in polished metal.

Not only that, but when you open an Apple product, it feels like an important event. You have to peel away the clear layers that keep anyone from handling the product until they've chosen to become its owner. Then you run your fingertip across the smooth surface. You feel the excitement of having purchased a quality product.

This experience is part of the education, whether you realize it or not. It's a tactile path to understanding that this product can change your life and that learning how to use it will allow you to be in life in a more efficient manner. It also subliminally tells you that this is something you need to take care of: "We at Apple have taken care of the way we package the product; you in return should take care of it."

Education is more than just instruction. It's about the implementation and strategies provided by the product.

It's about investing your time in the product because you believe it can change your life. Simplifying the complexities of how is where education can be incredibly effective.

The iPod, iPhone, and iPad are all intuitive. The education on the products is detailed toward emotion and how the product is going to change your life. Once you touch the product, intuition takes over. There is very little "how to" and an endless amount of education on when to use, where everything is on the product, within the product, how it's going to remember who you are, and how you will interact with it.

At the end of the day, it's a "sales" strategy targeted at the way you think versus the operational applications of the product. Genius.

THE RISE OF THE FRANKENBALL

The first TriggerPoint product I created—the Frankenball—was ultimately given a far sexier name: the TP Massage Ball. Despite refinements in production, it remained much the same as it had been at the outset: a conglomeration of several layers of materials that enabled the surface to change shape in five to seven seconds, depending on what was pressing against it.

This gave the ball the density of a thumb so that the feeling of contact with the ball felt just like a human hand. When you shut your eyes, it was easy to believe that a manual therapist was working on you.

For our customers, this product was incredibly sexy. Some, if any, were used to rolling golf balls or tennis balls around on their sore muscles and joints without any kind of purpose at all.

The TP Ball felt like they were doing something both strategic and targeted for themselves. Instead of the unfamiliar feeling of a hard golf ball or a fuzzy tennis ball on their skin, the sensation of the TP Ball made their body respond more intuitively. The muscular response was sure from the product, but it was really from the implementation strategies. The education created was a by-product of the innovations in use.

The product created efficiencies for personal care. We mirrored actions that a massage therapist and a physical therapist would do for you. We took the body through a range of motion and then took the product through specific ranges of motion. The two together created elasticity within the muscles, allowing for greater range of motion not only in the muscles but the surrounding muscles as well.

We would then educate you to compare the movement to other parts of your body so that you could understand the changes that were made. Remember, this company and its products were all created to empower a person to take care of themselves, relying on no one other than themselves.

Throughout this process, I never once had to tell them how cool the product was or show them pictures of sexy people using it, or compare its price to the cost of other alternatives.

All I had to teach them was how implementation could change their lives.

When I talked to my customers, I kept the conversation on biomechanics. I'd explain to them how the muscles in the lower leg influence the foot, and the foot is the first and last thing to hit the ground throughout the day.

Then I circled back and explained that the Achilles tendon is an anomaly. "It's the one thing that allows us to stand up straight. If you're not taking care of your posterior lower leg," I'd explain, "eventually you'll end up making a compromise. It's not a matter of how; it's a matter of when."

Once again, only after education on how to take care of themselves did I wrap the product in at the end as an implementation strategy.

It wasn't just our product that defined the industry; it was how we sold it. We applied that same strategy to every similar product we created for different areas of the body.

BUILT ON A SOLID FOUNDATION

Later on, I created a product called the Grid. This was in 2007, a time when foam rollers were becoming a commonplace item for athletes to use in muscle recovery. I've never liked foam rollers as they currently exist. I'd always say that they give you a false sense of security. It's like brushing your teeth with a T-shirt.

If you wanted to really change the way your body moved, TriggerPoint products were the only way to go. At the time, a foam roller was open-celled foam, a glorified swim noodle. There was no innovation, little education, and they were made of crappy foam, the leading material in landfills.

If I was going to create a "foam roller," I wanted to create a product that was sustainable, that did more than simply take advantage of a market. Remember, I don't like to follow. I like to lead, disrupt, get all eyes on what I'm doing. The Grid was hollow and used the least possible amount of foam. What made it work was that it had the texture of a meat tenderizer (which was an incredible innovation).

As you rolled over it, the Grid distributed blood and oxygen through the tissue of the muscles. We also ergonomically designed it so that the foot was always in a healthy position and your body was always low to the ground. And because it had a hard core inside, it offered firmer pressure while lasting longer and reducing the environmental impact at the end of its life.

The intention was never to sell this as a foam roller. We sold it as a device for core work combined with self-myofascial release. It was a way to "massage" the body and also get a core workout. It allowed us to stand out in the market and gave us a natural educational platform. In the end, the Grid family of products became roughly, at one point, 75 percent of our business.

We changed the way the world looked at self-massage and foam rolling. We were told that no one would ever pay $39.99 for this product. Now it's the industry standard. When you start as a premium product, make it better than anyone else, and justify the price based on quality, integrity, and trust. You can define cost, remain the industry thought leader, and pave the way for a family of products to be distributed.

It's really simple: make great products with great reasoning, get them into the right people's hands, and exploit the crap out of it when it happens. If you are built on a solid foundation, everything will be grand.

We truly redefined the way that the industry looked at a product because we started with an amazing product. If you're built on a false foundation, everything will come tumbling down.

SIMPLICITY IS THE FUTURE COMPLEXITY

Complexity accounts for most people's job security. In today's culture, keeping things mysterious and complex defines your company's need for your customer. They need to rely on you to take care of them.

If you have an attorney, you know what I'm talking about. When they speak, it's like a different language, and when they write, it's even worse. Estate planning is one of the most complicated things I've ever gone through. Once you start, it's like it never ends, leaving you with a hefty attorney bill and no way to explain what's been done. If you lose the attorney, you lose the brainchild to the complex organization of potential generations of assets.

Of course, there are now online platforms that streamline almost everything, from legal, HR, banking, and asset management to babysitting and dog-walking. I said from the very beginning that I wanted TriggerPoint to strip away the complexity and offer people simplicity instead. I wanted them to be able to take care of themselves, not need me to take care of them.

Typically, the physical therapy industries are complex by nature, which forces people to talk *at* you versus *to* you, due to insurance regulations. This can lead to frustrations and an inability to do things on your own or trust that you're even capable of doing things on your own.

THE SIMPLIFICATION OF WEB DESIGN

In the 1990s and the early 2000s, web designers suffered from overcomplexity. Websites and back-end design were so complex that they practically guaranteed that you had to rely on them for everything, even something as simple as uploading photos.

Today, however, web design has undergone a quantum shift, where the most competitive website platforms put the design power in the customer's hands. A great example is Wix, which turned the web design industry inside out by allowing you to not only create your own website through a template but essentially design it from scratch without having to know anything about code.

The future is user customization, and that means simplicity.

We now live in a world where complexity can ultimately lead to insanity because nothing works right. Amazon's server goes down, and we're all screwed. Our websites get hacked, and we lose our brand overnight.

For example, I recently bought a new home and put $25,000 worth of sound equipment into it. I have an operating system that's supposed to be able to control my lights, my TV, my projection screen, and all things electronic.

And of course it works perfectly every time, right? Hell no, it doesn't work.

I can't even turn the light switch on because it's controlled by this system. The technicians who come out to fix it every week have amazing job security—for now. There are so many times that I wish I had my old light switch back, a single universal remote, or even a simple battery rather than a USB plug.

It all comes back to simplicity. It's important for the integrity of your brand and the longevity of your business that you understand what your brand stands for and why. Make your brand messaging clear and simple. The more complicated it is, the more complicated it is to understand. Supply the need, and they will always come back for more; supply the want, and they will get confused and go with the next cheap product that comes their way.

Sure, there are some "want" brands that do well, but there are more "need" brands that expand and crush categories by keeping their brand messaging simple. There's a reason why staples such as Kleenex, GE, Apple, and Microsoft will never go away, no matter how advanced our society becomes. They will always fulfill a simple, true, and relevant need for consumers.

I'm not saying you should make something simple in the sense of being unsophisticated or crude. An iPhone or a website is anything but simple. But even the most complex product in the world can be explained in a very simple manner so that people can easily understand how to use it.

How easily you can explain your product directly coincides with how much of a necessity it is.

Expecting complexity to solve your problem is like taking fifty different remedies for a cold. You don't know what made you better, so you don't know what to take next time you get a cold.

The same rule applies in building your business.

This simplicity is the same principle that makes you part your hair on one side instead of the other or brush your teeth the same way. Somebody taught you to do it that way when you were a child, and you've done it the same way ever since.

You might choose to change your process over time, depending on what you learn or what you need. But the initial simplicity of that process is what allowed you to keep doing what you needed to do, over and over again, to take care of yourself.

Efficiencies come from repetition, and repetition is a by-product of memorable processes. This creates patterns, and patterns, in return, give you trust that you know what you're doing. Once the trust is built, the process becomes second nature. This not only creates a simple strategy from a potentially complex equation, but it also creates trust with yourself and builds integrity with the company, from core to extremity.

CHAPTER 10

WITH, NOT FOR

As a parent, I've always worried that my kids might develop a sense of entitlement. When my children reached the age where they could communicate their desires, I quickly decided to do things *with* my kids, not *for* my kids.

> ### ROMANS 12:8
>
> If it is to encourage, then give encouragement; if it is giving, then give generously; if it is to lead, do it diligently; if it is to show mercy, do it cheerfully.

The perfect example is when my son started skateboarding. He wasn't just cruising around the neighborhood. He was obsessed. He wanted more equipment and he wanted to spend all day using it.

I wanted to give him everything he wanted to make him happy in this new hobby. At the same time, I knew that giving him everything he wanted when he wanted it was a sure way to turn him into a brat. Instead, I gave him what he really needed: my involvement and collaboration in his new hobby.

I started skateboarding with him, and we got an instructor to coach us. (My son was way better than I was, but he appreciated the effort I was putting into it.) I had someone build a half-pipe in the backyard so we could skate at home together. I got so into it that I ended up making it my goal to complete a drop-in by the time I turned forty-five. It took a lot of practice and a lot of bumps and bruises, but on my forty-fifth birthday, I dropped in and was able to hold it. That was a big milestone for me and for my son. It became more than just a hobby for him. It gave us an emotional bond.

My other son is completely different. He has a marginal interest in sports and is more of a video game guy. I had to work harder to find a way to relate with him since athletics are my natural bent. He was really into a game called Skylanders, so I memorized about twenty-five different Skylander characters so I could rattle off their names at any time. He was so happy to share any interest with me that he absolutely blossomed.

KEEP UP, OR WE'LL COACH YOU OUT

It's amazing to tell this story and compare it to the mindset I had when I started my family. I'm a product of the old-school family man mindset: "If I buy you what you want, you should appreciate me." A lot of times in marriage, that's the equation we concentrate on. "Look what you have. Look what I've done for you. How can you complain?" But what your significant other wants in life is your undivided attention. They want you to listen to what they're going through and to be interested in their day, not just hear you spout off everything you've done for them.

Once I started to recognize this, I realized that I should be treating my employees the same way. This was a huge revelation for me: treat your employees like people, do things *with* them and not *for* them, and they might actually do things for the company you never thought possible. That's when this epiphany of "with, not for" became the most relevant thing in employee management that I could have ever stumbled upon.

From the perspective of any employer, I gave my employees a lot: I paid for their insurance, I put a CrossFit gym in our office, I paid for a trainer to come train everybody, and I brought in lunch the days that we worked out as a group.

But even while providing all these perks, I still wasn't available to my employees for genuine communication. I didn't take time to get to know a lot of my employees because I was running so fast. My perspective was totally misguided by my desire to move fast: either keep up, or we'll coach you out. Unfortunately, that environment is a breeding ground for animosity.

If I could do it all over again, I would have spent more time sitting *beside* my employees instead of *across* from them. I would have talked *with* them, not *at* them.

I would have done things *with* them, not *for* them.

THE BALANCE OF POWER

If your company grows to the point where you're not doing the hiring anymore, you may look up one day and see your office full of people you don't know.

At this level, you probably don't have the daily contact with your employees that allows you to get to know them. At that point, you have to create a top-down perspective of "with, not for." You have to spend more quality time with your managers to set the tone for them to do the same with individual employees.

If you really want the best out of your employees, you've

got to institutionalize the principle of "with, not for." You can't just do an open forum, throw them a pizza party, or stack their contract with benefits and then expect that they'll always be loyal to you and the business.

Any job, even with great perks, ends in burnout when it isn't sustained by the "with, not for" principle. It doesn't take much from you as a boss. Just a willingness to sit down and get to know your employees.

What are they interested in? Do they have siblings? What is their favorite movie? Where do they like to vacation? Ask these questions rather than the typical ones about where they want to go in your company, what their career goals are, and how you can help them get there. If you don't prioritize working *with* your employees, they will only be working *for* you. In today's culture, that kind of job has a limited shelf life.

It is imperative to work with your employees so that they understand your expectations. By seeing how you work, they can understand your thought processes. Now, I want to be clear: this is not so that they perform a task just like you do. Rather, it's to help them know how you think and how you communicate.

People want to be treated like people, and as an entrepreneur, you are in the people business even if you don't really like people.

WHY THE BEST EMPLOYEES LEAVE

Employees have it tough in the workplace, especially if they don't have a voice, a purpose, or an understanding of what the employer wants and where their employer wants the company to go.

This is why the best employees end up leaving or getting fired: they never get a chance to show what they're capable of. If someone comes in with a world of potential, you have to foster that potential. Be willing to teach, educate, and mold their thought processes into the best possible employee for the brand.

No one wants to be talked at. They want to be spoken with. The only way you can master this is by caring about your employees and doing things *with* them, not *for* them.

That's what made all the difference in the world in my relationship with my sons. I could have held the parental "perks" over their heads and squeezed them for every last ounce of praise they had to give. Instead, I took an interest in them *as people*, not just as my kids, and we created a stronger bond than ever. Show up to work every day with the goal of showing your employees that you're interested in who they are, not what you can do for each other.

Here is a process I created once I realized some employees needed more than just an email every now and again.

THE 3/2 RULE

One of my biggest frustrations as the CEO of Trigger-Point was the tendency for employees to surrender to excuses. They'd say, "That's not my job" or "I don't know what I'm supposed to be doing." We'd hire somebody for a job in marketing, and within six months, I'd find them working in product development.

I'd track them down and ask, "What's going on here? What are you doing? Your job is in marketing."

They'd say, "Yeah, I know. But I really want to contribute to product development."

When your company is small, sure, everyone contributes to everything. As you grow, though, you've got to narrow down everyone's lane so that each employee knows what they are supposed to be doing.

A key part of balance, one that is often overlooked, is the fulcrum. If you don't have a solid, reliable base, no amount of counterweight can keep you in balance. For the employees who decided to drift into other departments, they'd shifted their fulcrum, thinking that they brought the same skills to any position in the company. They may have even thought that by drifting from one department to another, they were doing us a favor. Wasn't it good that they were following their passion?

In the case of a growing company, it's not good for the team for people to shift their fulcrum.

Think about it: with two people in the company, balance is easy to manage.

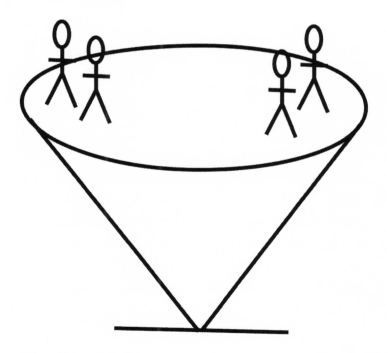

As you add four to six people, it becomes more difficult to stabilize everyone on the base or fulcrum.

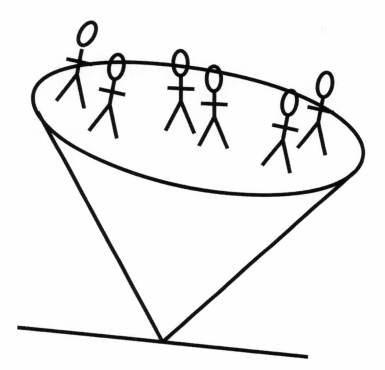

Once you get to fifty employees, everyone should be balanced and moving fast, much like a spinning top. When all employees know what they are doing, why they are doing it, and how they should be engaging with all other departments, that top can spin incredibly fast. When people get out of their lane, it throws the balance off, and the top wobbles hopelessly. In the end, you start losing people because no one knows what the hell they are supposed to be doing.

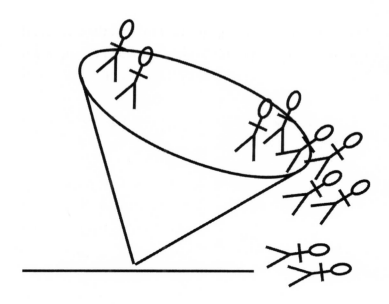

This is why I came up with my 3/2 rule.

I'd bring an employee into my office, hand them a marker, and say, "OK, write three things on the whiteboard that you're good at."

They'd write their three things, perhaps *writing, design, and creativity*.

"Now," I'd say, "write two things on the board that you're *great* at."

They'd think for a minute—greatness is a bold claim—then write their two qualities on the board: *strategy and operations*.

We'd step back and look at the words on the board. I'd take the marker and draw a line between them, much like a fraction—three words over two. Then I'd ask them,

"Why are you doing the things that you're good at? I hired you for the things that you're great at!"

Sometimes they'd get it right away, but often, we'd sit down to talk about it. It takes longer to do what you're good at than it does to do what you're great at. Longer hours spent working creates mental and physical challenges for employees. At TriggerPoint, on countless occasions, the job confusion came from their own inner drive to prove something to someone.

In many cases, these employees had a similar history as me. They'd often open up to me and admit that there was someone in their past who had told them they couldn't do certain things, just like I'd experienced.

> **PROVERBS 27:17**
>
> As iron sharpens iron, a friend sharpens a friend.

"I don't need you to prove anything to me," I'd tell them. "I'm completely convinced that you have potential for greatness. That's why I hired you. When you're ignoring the things you're *great* at to spend time on the things you're *good* at, you're not pleasing those people who underestimated you or proving them wrong. You're just letting their judgments influence your life."

There are two personality tests that I've found to be incredibly illuminating in the hiring process: behavioral insights from http://Birkman.com/ and the DISC profile test at TonyRobbins.com/disc/.

Ever wonder why some of your friends have stayed in school forever, doing one graduate program after another? It could be because they're great at learning but horrible at implementing. And it's not hard to see why.

Bringing something to fruition is scary. From the moment you stop saying, "I'm learning to do this," and say, "I *am* doing this," you're inviting judgment from your colleagues and peers, your competition, and even your family.

Nobody likes to be judged. Staying just *good* at something is a place that's relatively safe from judgment. But aiming for greatness exposes you.

CHAPTER 11

THE EYE OF OPPORTUNITY

If you've been paying attention along the way, you know by now that passionate entrepreneurs set out to build the next great brand by using all of their life experiences to inform their decision. Everything that you've gone through, good and bad, will be part of what forms the greatness of your future.

However, you have to choose which of these things to put together in forming those unbreakable bonds.

Think about it in terms of forming your own personality. As you grow up, nature and nurture together give you equal parts of your mother and father. Cross their personalities, physical traits, and genetic makeup, and that's you. You're essentially the Venn diagram of your parents. If you are too much like one or the other, you typically end up using those traits as an excuse to act a certain way.

"Well, my father did it, so I do too."

"My mother acted that way, so why should I act any differently?"

To get that balance, with equal parts of your personality overlapping one another, it may take some work. If you put in the work, everyone in your life will benefit.

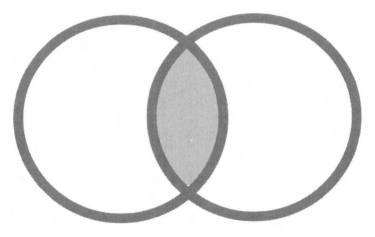

Throughout your life, reality checks will reveal not only who and what you are but also how you became that way based on who and what your parents are. If you're willing to look honestly at the good and the bad, you can then accurately look through all those elements—good and bad alike—and clearly see the opportunity for you to take action to become who and what you want to be.

The beauty of business is that it works very much that same way. When you take equal parts education and instruction and overlap them, you have your eye of opportunity for marketing. When you overlap marketing with education, you create the eye of sales opportunity.

The essence of the Venn diagram is to keep what you are doing in check. There are two sides to every equation, and there are two sides to every great relationship. As the two sides overlap, there is inevitably an eye that is created by the overlap. This eye should always be the focus for greatness, even when you combine more than one area.

Here's an example:

Marketing, sales, education, information—if you take 25 percent of each of these areas to overlap, this is going to create a brand strategy. One area can influence the other. If it doesn't, then the Venn diagram will be out of balance, and your messaging will be confusing to the customer.

It's crazy when you think this way, as you can also apply it to your employees. Each employee in those departments should be overlapping with other employees in the other departments just enough to create an unbreakable bond. Just like muscles are to act independent yet as one, so are your employees.

GIVE PEOPLE WHAT THEY NEED, NOT ONLY WHAT THEY WANT

People need certain things in their life. They need health, they need their will to live, and they need safety. But, my gosh, do they *want* so much more than that.

I believe that fulfilling their *needs* makes people *want* more. There is typically a desired outcome that is accompanied by a need—I need food so I can get nutrients, I need shelter so I don't die in the elements, and I need water so I don't dehydrate—but wants stem from an infatuation with things.

You can live without a want, but you can't live without a need. If you can make people believe that your brand, product, knowledge, education, or service is something they can't live without and if you present it to them in a way that allows them to learn (versus talking down to them), you've got a window of opportunity to empower someone into making a purchasing decision, taking an employment opportunity, or getting behind your brand in a huge way.

When it comes to fulfilling what people need from me, I recommend the 80/20 rule.

As a parent, 80 percent of what I give my kids is fulfilling their needs, while only 20 percent is for wants.

This principle of "need versus want" also comes back to you as the entrepreneur leading this company. What you *want* is to succeed, impress people, and make millions of dollars. But what *really* compelled you to start this particular business in the first place? What itch did you need to scratch? What people did you need to help because nobody else was doing it?

Throughout the life span of your company, you have to keep coming back to this central need because the closer you stick to it, the more successful you'll be. Your need will point you in the direction you need to go.

TISSUE PAPER OR FIDGET SPINNERS—PICK ONE

You need tissue paper to wipe your nose, clean your hands, and of course, clean your backside. These are true needs in my book; therefore, Kleenex will always be around.

But how about a fidget spinner. Every kid in America wanted a fidget spinner in 2017. These things popped up out of nowhere, and they left the world just as fast as they came into it. The want was so great that you'd pay fifty dollars for one when they first came out. But twelve months later, they were sold for ninety-nine cents at every gas station across America.

The needed company, Kleenex, maintains their brand, while the wanted company never actually had a brand. They just had a product.

Personally, my need in life is to empower others. When I get that, I am so emotionally and physically charged that it's unbelievable. That's how I recognize it's a true need within me. In addition, I know that I need my faith, family, and friends.

Now, I may *want* to be a race car driver or to make more money or to do any number of other things, but they won't fulfill me in the same way I'm fulfilled when my *needs* are met. Moreover, if I focus on pursuing those wants, I'll forget about the things I need.

NEEDS AND WANTS IN BUSINESS

As an entrepreneur, it is imperative to refine your thought process so that needs are priorities and wants are secondary. This especially becomes a problem once you receive an infusion of capital. I see so many people who, as soon as they get into a position of influence and power, go get everything they ever *wanted*.

They forget about the need for infrastructure and process; instead, they go out and hire a marketing or PR company, get new employees, or develop new products in the lineup, all because they want their company to seem bigger and more put together than it actually is. In return, they compromise their company by trying to grow too fast.

What they really needed to do was refine the product, improve the messaging, and connect with the brand and the end user. We all want to be a big deal and influence people, but what we really need is to listen, learn, and implement strategies that are for the greater good of the brand, employees, sales, marketing, process, and of course, your end users.

I believe that there is a portion of society that lives with a *want* mentality, but they struggle to manage their needs. This is a scary place to be. If you chase the wants, you end up turning around one day and finding that you're bankrupt and have nobody around you who cares about you. Whereas if you just simply sit back and do an honest reality check about who and what you are, you'll have the ability to say, "Here are my needs: I need to be loved, I need to be supported, I need to change the world."

You can absolutely achieve those things, but it's a process. However, once you recognize that the goal or product you're working for is a need, you'll do whatever it takes to work through the challenges to reach it.

Wants, on the other hand, are easy come, easy go.

It takes more time and effort to be a need-based company, but if your company truly fulfills a need, you'll have every opportunity to stick around for a long time and potentially change the world.

THE EYE OF OPPORTUNITY—YOU, YOUR EMPLOYEES, AND YOUR CUSTOMERS

If you're snorting cocaine, drinking booze, and chasing ladies all day, you're fulfilling all your wants, but you're still a zero. You're not fulfilling any of your true needs, and if you look honestly at who and what you are, you'll be aware of that.

The same thing is true regarding the needs of your business. Are you *really* looking at the needs of this business, and are they being met? If they are, you create an unbreakable bond, not only between you and your employees but also with the customer as a third part of the bond.

However, if you're self-absorbed and focused only on the

things you want for your business—more money, more employees, a wider range of products, better market share—your brand will suffer. On top of that, you'll just be lonely. When you throw all your focus and effort into things that don't have a need tied into it, you will run out of money, potentially lose your company, and throw away your opportunity to change the world.

Your brand is defined by understanding how you're answering the needs of those who are out there in the world. You are not branding a product. You are branding what will change the life of your customer.

If you really want to create an unbreakable bond between your company and the customer, you've got to truly address whatever it is that you're doing as a need in their life. If you do that and you meet a specific price point, there's no denying that you'll have a customer for life. You've redefined what it is that they need, and their life will never be the same.

QUESTIONS TO REFINE YOUR BRAND PERSPECTIVE

- What is the purpose-driven path of the brand/company?
- Whom will you be taking care of?
- Where is the need for your brand versus your desire to be a big company?

The purpose-driven path of TriggerPoint was to empower those who were in need of better movement, whether their restrictions were the by-product of an injury, they were getting old, or they hadn't lived an active lifestyle in a long time. We wanted to educate people so they could understand what was going on with their body and why, and in turn, they could share that knowledge with others.

A need-based, purpose-driven path will guide you through the times when everything seems to be going against you.

LEAD WITH THE NEED

I talked earlier about the Grid, a hollow foam roller I created in 2007. We applied for a patent on it, but those can take years to come through. In the meantime, an infinite number of other brands were taking advantage of what we had done and creating knockoffs of our product.

Their subpar products were devaluing our product in the marketplace.

Everybody likes to say that imitation is the greatest form of flattery. To them, I say, "Yeah, until *you* get knocked off." For me, it was a huge accomplishment to come up with a product that was truly unique in a world where there are very few truly unique things. To then be taken advantage of and disrespected by others in my market-place was incredibly painful.

Those copycat companies didn't lead with a need. They didn't understand the purpose-driven path. Their philosophy (if you can call it that) was to simply take advantage of the trend for as long as they could and then disappear with the money they made. There was no integrity.

That is technically a business strategy, and by some estimates, it might be a good one. It's just not for me. I want to create a customer *for life*, not take advantage of customers by producing a low-cost piece of crap product that they buy because it looks the same as the expensive one. These companies are bottom feeders, scum of the earth, con artists.

No matter what, integrity is powerful. You don't create integrity by being a copycat and ripping people off. You act with integrity when you find a need that people don't have fulfilled, and you do everything in your power to help serve that need. That's how you get straight to the eye of opportunity that fulfills the needs of you, your employees, and your customers, all at the same time.

CHAPTER 12

EXIT STRATEGY

If you continue down the purpose-driven path for long enough, you'll reach a point where you'll need to move on. Mind you, an exit has more meaning than just selling your business. You have to think about what you want as an entrepreneur, sure, but you also have to consider your needs as a person.

- Are you at your best in your current business?
- Are you enjoying the ride?
- Are you excited about every single day you spend at work?

Most entrepreneurs are control freaks. We don't like allowing someone else too much power over any area of our business. We like to say it's because they'll screw up our vision, but deep down inside, this is really because we don't know how to communicate our vision and expectations with other people.

We don't know how to hold people accountable, so we just hold on tight. If you're not careful, you might choke your business out. Looking out for the future of your company means building something that can work *without* depending on you for everything.

Most entrepreneurs have a codependent relationship with their company. With no goals or strategies for a future exit, you end up going into the office every day without a plan because you want the crap to hit you, versus having it hit the fan. You feel better when there is a problem than when there isn't one. This is unhealthy but common.

Figure out a way to set goals on an annual, quarterly, monthly basis. Then use these as benchmarks of success. Don't be afraid of success or setting your company up for an exit.

If you still have that "everything depends on me" mentality, by the time your company really starts to take off, it will throw the balance of your company off-kilter. Your employees will hate you because you're not letting them do their job or exercise their creativity. Your family will hate you because you're never at home. And if the day comes when you want to exit the company, you'll find yourself in a place where your exit means the end of the brand.

But if you instead recognize that the company will reach a day when it doesn't need you anymore—and you realize that's a good thing—you can take a step back to create plans to prepare for the moment you do walk off into the sunset.

FIND YOUR WOZNIAK

As you grow bigger as a business and prepare your company for your own exit—whether years or decades away—you'll be faced with a harsh truth: you're only as good as your team.

Each team member has to rely on one another, and that dependency has to be built on trust.

A big part of building trust is trusting people to help you. I believe every entrepreneur has some kind of learning disability or super ability (depending on your perspective). You can look back at business history and see that many of the geniuses were dyslexic, ADD or ADHD, obsessive-compulsive—you name it.

Their so-called disabilities are what gave them freedom to look outside of the box. However, somebody always had to come in and be the Steve Wozniak to the Steve Jobs, so to speak, creating the process for the genius's unconventional passions.

As I've said, I've always been horrible at communicating. I can talk you deaf, dumb, and blind about the abstract of something, but when it comes to the linear side of things, I suck. I'm still trying to be diligent about details, but I'm not much better at it now than I was when TriggerPoint first started.

The day I decided to get a personal assistant changed everything for me. It took all the things that I wasn't good at off my plate, allowing me to focus on my passion.

When you have a process-oriented person assisting you in your life, and they're someone who really gets who and what you are, they can build the process for taking care of yourself into your life. Things such as scheduling calls, returning emails, making doctors' appointments (and making sure you go), setting up a dinner date with your wife—being able to delegate all those details takes a huge weight off your shoulders.

I'll admit that it was difficult at first to allow someone else to do these mundane things for me. I was afraid that people would judge me for needing help at this level. But the truth was that if I didn't have somebody else supporting me through scheduling and regulating, I would never even think about those things until it was too late.

When I allowed my assistant to help me this way, it was liberating, like getting a cast off my arm. By making myself vulnerable to my assistant and asking for support where I was weak, I had created a shield of protection for those weaknesses.

Don't be afraid to be successful. Don't be afraid to put certain measures in place that successful people do to make sure that you hit all your timelines and objectives. Don't be afraid to show other people your success by having them manage and regulate the things that you forget about. It's pretty simple. Don't be afraid—not of asking for help, not to sell your company. Fear nothing.

NOBODY WANTS A FOUNDER-DEPENDENT COMPANY

Just like you have to be vulnerable to an assistant, you have to do the same to those who are within your executive team. I mentioned earlier in the book that you should hire for your weaknesses, hire to gain additional strengths, but most importantly, surround yourself with executives who believe in your vision.

Allow each person to do what they do great, and everyone

will kick ass together. I love relying on others to get crap done. I also love when those others let me know what they have done. Support those who support you, and you'll create an incredible infrastructure.

Most founders and creative CEOs suck at process, yet they have an overflow of passion. So find your operations person, COO, manager, and director; share with them all that you want to accomplish; and let them do it. If you are the only one who knows everything in your company and you don't trust anyone, you're in trouble.

No one wants to acquire a company that is so founder-dependent that nothing happens without his or her knowledge. This type of situation puts too much stress on a company pre and post sale.

Admit that you need help and find people to mitigate your weaknesses. Your exit strategy depends on it.

PLANNING *YOUR* EXIT STRATEGY

If you go into your business from day one with an exit strategy, you need to really think about what you're doing—it's a sure sign that you're process-driven, not passion-driven.

But for most entrepreneurs, the exit strategy is not even

a blip on their radar. And their books are clear evidence of that. They've been living out of the business since the day they started it, writing everything off.

That's fine if you're running a lifestyle brand that you expect to hold on to for the rest of your life until you die in the saddle. But if your business is product-oriented, you have to realize that the nature of your product and even your industry are going to change. You can't guarantee that what you do now will be what you do in twenty years.

That's why you need to have a plan in place for why, when, and how you'll exit someday.

Once you become a successful business, you have to start treating your books as though you could exit tomorrow. The process you put in place to clean up your books will not only set you in order for the day that you decide to exit, but it will also increase the value of your company by offering standards and processes for efficiency that everyone can understand.

THE WHY

One of the biggest problems with an exit strategy is figuring out why you're doing it.

Where are you in life? How long has the business been

around? What's the value? How do you define the value? For the entrepreneur, it's all about evaluating *emotional* dollars, while the purchaser is simply evaluating the physical dollars.

This is where taking care of yourself along the way will really help. If you stop, pull back, and start to take care of yourself within your business, you won't put yourself in an impossible situation of wanting to exit but not being able to get the price you want.

If you're living with your nose to the grindstone, trying to handle everything yourself, you won't have that thousand-foot view that allows you to make an informed or healthy decision about your exit strategy. Taking care of yourself along the way gives you the mental space to consider your business's value accurately.

ASK YOURSELF...

- Do I want to do this for the rest of my life?
- Do I want to pass my business down to my children?
- Do I want to pass it on to my employees?
- If I want to sell the business, have I thought about when?
- Are my financials in a place that would allow a purchaser to understand all of my expenses, receivables, and assets?

THE WHEN

In the beginning of your business, your finger is on the pulse of the industry. You're tracking every change in the market so that you can position yourself for success.

You need to maintain (or redevelop) that eagle-eye view of your industry when you're at the other end of the spectrum. Always be aware of where you are in the business and where the business is within the market.

When I started TriggerPoint, all I wanted to do was empower people to take care of themselves and do things they never thought possible with the therapy I'd found. For the first three years, the only thing holding that business together was passion. But as we started to become successful, it occurred to me that we needed some process.

Later, I realized that I wasn't performing a role in my company that corresponded to my passion. By the same token, my company wasn't playing the same role it used to in the market. Both had changed around me in a way that didn't let me fulfill my passion through TriggerPoint anymore. That was my first big clue that it was time to start considering an exit.

When you notice your passion is no longer being fulfilled by the company and that the company is fulfilling a need in an industry you're no longer intimate with, it may be time to either reengage or choose an exit time.

THE HOW

The best-case scenario for your exit is getting an offer from someone else to buy the company from you. Having your books in order will greatly help with the transition. When someone comes along with an interest in acquiring your business, the first place they'll look is your books.

Simply put, if your books aren't in order, you're not a purchasable entity.

It's just like selling your house: no matter how many warm memories you have of it or how valuable it has been in your life, you won't be able to sell it at its full value if the landscaping is torn up or the carpet is full of mud.

The cleaner your books are, the more you'll be able to sell the business for. People will trust you. They'll see you have nothing to hide. In addition, clean books allow people to plainly see the successes of your company as well as the failures and the challenges.

Moreover, keeping clean books throughout your business's life will allow you to see the same challenges a potential buyer would see and address them accurately.

But if your books require your buyer to dig through and find the holes themselves, you've lost leverage.

WHEN IGNORANCE STOPPED BEING BLISSFUL

When I was ready to sell TriggerPoint, I had yet another abrupt reality check. I was used to coming in to work in jeans and a black T-shirt. Casual dress had become just as much a part of my brand as the logo.

However, when I sat down with the people who were interested in acquiring the company, they interpreted my attire very differently.

Bear in mind, this was before the Silicon Valley boom, when powerful people started wearing hoodies and slippers or workout clothes and five-toe shoes to the office of the most profitable companies in the world. At that time, casual dress in a high-profile business meeting read as disrespect.

As I say, ignorance is bliss—right up until you get called on it. They looked at me and thought, *This is all we're worth to you? You couldn't clean up for an important meeting?*

I hadn't put any thought into this aspect of my exit strategy. I hadn't considered how I could communicate well to potential buyers of my company. So right after that meeting, I went to Nordstrom's and spent thousands of dollars on a ton of dress clothes.

In order to accomplish my goal of selling the business I'd created, I essentially had to rebrand myself. From that moment on, I presented myself in meetings as an organized, intentional, knowledgeable person so that an acquirer might feel comfortable and confident about who and what I was.

They looked at me in my suit and designer shoes and saw someone who cared what he looked like, which to them communicated me as someone who cared about the brand he'd created. I think that played as big a role in the success of exiting my company as the orderly financials I presented.

I never realized before that I had a codependency on my business. The brand was me, and I was the brand for the longest time. Now I was spending all my time trying to convince others that the brand could live beyond me, that the brand was bigger than me, that not having me around wouldn't hold back the business under someone else's leadership.

This was an expected obstacle to selling the business. What I never expected was the *pain.*

It was almost as emotionally challenging as a divorce. Yes,

I walked away with a lot of money from the deal, but as we all know, money doesn't make you happy. Money makes the happy times in your life really happy, and it makes the sad times really sad because you can buy anything you want and it still doesn't change your emotions at their core.

For me, the success of TriggerPoint was the American dream playing out in my life. I built a business out of the back of my car to earning somewhere close to $70 million by the time I left. It was unbelievable. It had made me who and what I'd wanted to become. Leaving it behind was emotionally complicated.

THE BITTERSWEET CELEBRATION

The day I sold TriggerPoint, I walked into the office and said, "Hey, uh, well...the thing that all you guys have been stressing out about, it happened. And because it happened, I'd like everybody to meet me at the bar tonight, and we're all going to party like rock stars."

And party we did. All the employees at TriggerPoint came out, and we partied. But as we partied, I couldn't help asking myself as I looked around, *Are these my actual friends? I've been regarding them as family, but are they? Are they happy for me? Are they sad that I'm leaving? Are they jealous? Are they concerned about the brand's future? I don't know how I should act. Should I be elated because now I've got a bunch of money in my pocket?*

But if I didn't care about all those people, I wouldn't feel all those emotions. We did something amazing together, and now we were parting ways, having done something special.

Selling your business is an emotionally complicated decision, and it can take longer than a few nights and more than a few beers to sort through those emotions. Give yourself time.

KNOWING WHEN IT'S TIME

Choosing when to sell forces you to straddle a fine line between leaving a little money on the table and holding on for too long. You want to get out with your financial freedom, but you also want a return on the investment you've made. In the meantime, the brand, the market, and everything else start to devalue.

HOW TO RUN AN ANNUAL ASSESSMENT

As important as it is to assess who and what your company is, it's essential to do a yearly assessment on who and what you want your company to be.

- Is this year the year we start to leverage our brand into an exit?
- What is the market saying?
- Where is the greatest return?
- When is our best time to begin moving toward an exit? Is it today? Is it a year from now?
- Are we the market leader? If yes, how leverageable is the brand? If no, what would it take to get the company there?
- Am I the thought leader in the space?

There's no perfect time to sell your business. It's just like the time that you fell in love. You never expected it to happen, but when the moment came, you surrendered to it. Your emotional connection with your business will let you know when it's time to let it go.

You want to sell it at a point where all cylinders are firing. Leverage the good times to get a great price. There are so many people who are waiting to see what's on the other side of the rainbow only to find that the downward curve of the rainbow was their market share.

I am a big believer that you should sell on the climb, as you never know where the plateau may come. If you're waiting for the perfect moment but you see a decrease in sales or market share, that means the blue skies are gone. You've waited too long.

You will always be emotionally connected to your business. Even if you no longer own it, the emotions are essentially the same. It's like your child going off to college. Yes, they're off on their own following their own dreams, but you still feel a deep connection with them.

For me, TriggerPoint stopped being sexy when we stopped talking about helping people. Instead, we were talking all the time about numbers and increasing margins. We had products all over the world and a huge team of employees, contractors, and distributors.

We were living the dream, but the person I cared about the most—the customer—was getting lost in the shuffle. My passion was for the people who dealt with chronic pain, the people who needed a greater quality of life.

But we started sacrificing the passion for the person for the process of the dollar.

HOW TO USE AN ADJUSTED EBITA TO BUILD VALUE FOR YOUR COMPANY

When it comes to creating your exit strategy, being strategic is a lot better than being exhausted. Every year, you should look at all the different variables—your goals for the business, your family and personal life, the sacrifices you're making, and the emotional and financial payoff—and use those variables to make a strategic decision around continuing forward or planning an exit.

That decision comes down to one of two things. You can either increase your revenue so that you can diversify the company and/or put more money in your pocket, or you can increase your EBITA (earnings before interest, taxes, and amortization) so that you get a higher multiple from a strategic or private equity.

You always have to be looking at your product offering, when the right time to sell is, and when the right time to decrease costs is. Another option is asking whether it's time to market the crap out of your company and lower your EBITA because you're building a brand. There is a lot of value in taking this approach, as you can always try to use an adjusted EBITA to come up with the value of your company.

Bottom line, it was just time. Every entrepreneur can feel it when this moment arrives. Whether they choose to act on it or not is up to them. Everybody can say they have the best strategy to purchase or sell a stock, or acquire a company, but at the end of the day, it's all based on your gut feeling.

When I had my production management company in Los Angeles, I still remember standing in a doorway when one of my partners was rattling off who we were about to raise money from, why it was important, and the role that each member of the company was going to take. I actually remember telling myself, *Don't do it. This isn't the right investor*, and I still did it because it was easy. In the end, I got kicked out of the company by the same person who was putting the deal together.

Trust your gut, people.

REMEMBER, THERE'S NO GOING BACK

Sacrifice is part of building anything. If your sacrifice isn't required, there's nothing for you to gain. I sacrificed so much when building TriggerPoint: I was away from my kids up to eight months out of the year, and I was lucky to have a marriage based on the way I treated my wife for so many years. I was an occasional father and a half-assed husband—not because I *wanted* to be but because I *needed* to be to get the company where it wound up!

Now, after the sale, it was my responsibility to refill the buckets and be the best parent and husband I possibly could.

Ultimately, we pursue money for a reason, and you need to be clear about what that reason is. Do you want to travel the world? Do you want to make out with your wife every day? Do you want to be a better parent? Do you want to be a philanthropist?

Whatever your desire with your money, make sure you actually follow through once your exit is complete. It's the only thing that helps you through the emotional roller coaster of disconnecting with your entrepreneurial identity.

You've put in years of emotional vulnerability with this company—building it has made you who and what you are—and it's no longer a presence in your life. Stepping away won't be easy, but you can make it easier by *actually stepping away*—completely.

TriggerPoint was a true testament to my purpose-driven path. It was exactly what I was supposed to be doing from 2002 to 2014. It validated me as a person, as a visionary, as a businessperson, and as a CEO. But life moves on.

As you sell your business and life continues, you will still always think about your business—the hard yards, the elation, the vulnerable emotions. But my hope for you is that you can look in your heart (and your pocket) and feel validated that you did it your way. My hope for you is that you are able to refill your faith and family buckets now that you've got the funds in the bank.

Remember, nobody cares how hard you work or how

much money you have, but people do care if you are a good person.

Give thanks to everyone around you, reward all of their efforts, and never second-guess your decisions. You can always try to stack your money pile and compare it to someone else's. If that's the game you want to play.

But nobody—and I mean *nobody*—can stack their experiences to compare to yours. You've lived your life, and I've lived mine. My only hope is that this book of my experiences helps to make your life a little better.

CONCLUSION

ENJOYING THE REWARDS

When it comes to the final act of your entrepreneurial journey—whether in a specific business or in your career— your last action as a leader is defining and offering reward. People who supported you along the way will be looking to you to define and provide the reward for their service.

Reward is such a relative term.

It depends largely on how you ran your company and managed the employees under you. If you ran your company purely on process and defined success along the way solely in terms of finance, you've set a precedent for how your employees will define reward. At that point, no matter what you give them, it might not ever meet their expectations. In my experience, people who define reward in terms of money always want more. That's just the way it works.

The same is true of how you reward yourself. It's hard to say while you're in the trenches what reward will feel like at the end. How much money and glory will feel like adequate repayment for all you've sacrificed along the way?

The legacy you leave to your company is one thing. You can exit that company and never have to talk to those people again. But the legacy you've created within your home life will stay with you forever.

The sacrifices that you made while building your business will have to be not only rewarded but also repaid. You have to be grateful to your family for their support, but you also have to be willing to change. You have to relearn how to contribute in the areas you neglected, how to be available emotionally as well as physically.

These rewards may sound like a lot of reparations to make for other people, but ultimately, they are rewards you offer *yourself*. These rewards are much richer if you put in the hard yards of building discipline through habits, finding support for your weaknesses, and constantly improving your communication.

You should know that as you put in those efforts, it will feel as though you work for your employees instead of the other way around. Over time, though, you'll be able to see the reality is that you all work together. Feeling comfortable is not a destination. It's a milestone that demands both celebration and reevaluation.

Ultimately, you have to do what you do for yourself, not for others. Being gracious and giving makes a difference to your employees and in how you run your business, but it makes the most difference in your own life. Not only will those two qualities help you build your business's success, but they will also allow you to look back on your career and feel comfortable with the decisions you made.

My greatest hope in writing this book is to help entrepreneurs understand that being an entrepreneur is one of the most fulfilling pursuits in life. It's an amazing experience, right up there with falling in love for the first time. But just as in love, being passionate about something doesn't ensure that everything will work out successfully.

Success is based off the contribution, the vulnerability, the willingness to listen, the unwavering commitment to every attempt you make. Passion can be an overpowering emotion sometimes forcing you to do things that are not the smartest ways to get things done.

Surround yourself with great people who also want to lead, listen, learn, and build something amazing. For some, it might be dollars, others will want a lifestyle, but regardless of the cash in the bank or the emotional currency, make sure to appreciate all those who are around you having to deal with the emotional roller coaster you call the entrepreneurial life.

You've made infinite sacrifices along the way. Be aware of each bucket (area) of your life you've already sacrificed: faith, family, and health. You could have all the money in the world, but if you're fat, depressed, have no relationship with your kids, and your husband or wife left a long time ago, then what was the point?

REMEMBER...

- Strengthen your strengths and hire for your weaknesses.
- Passion before process.
- Money can make you stupid.
- A healthy body is a healthy mind.
- Trust your gut.
- To be who you want to be in life, you have to accept where you are today.
- Everything that happened in the past makes you perfect for today, tomorrow, and the days to come. Use your experience to communicate clearly.
- Listen, learn, and care for those who are around you. Care for who they are, not just what they can do for you.

The entrepreneurial spirit is all about building processes that allow your passion to thrive. If you can pursue that spirit in the earliest stage of your business, you'll be able to take the greatest risks that lead to the financial freedom you hope for.

Even in your next venture.

How do you get there, even after you've moved on from your first company? Every three to five years, you have to circle back to the reality check that started this whole book.

- Who and what are you?
- Where are you starting from?
- Why are you here?
- What do you want?
- How will you get there?

You've got to work hard to be unaffected by the challenges of owning your own business. Be a leader for all those who are around you, allow them to follow in the wake of your passion. Build processes for your *entire life* so that you leave no one behind in this wonderful world of entrepreneurship. It's entirely possible to walk your entire path without ever realizing the stress, frustration, and anger you have internally. Recognize those emotions first, and then account for them.

If you learn nothing else from this book, take this away: if you have to think about being an entrepreneur, then don't do it!

But if you want to be an entrepreneur, beyond a shadow of a doubt, go all the way in and never look back. If you accept yourself for who you are, you can constantly adapt so you can be who you want to be in the future.

There are plenty of things you can control here on earth, but I still believe you should have faith beyond yourself and belief in the power of selflessness and a lack of judgment for those around you.

Work efficiently, communicate effectively, and appreciate all those who help you achieve your purpose. I have done everything good in my life through my faith. I hope that you find yours too.

I will leave you with this one thought: When you die and your children are standing at the podium for your funeral, how do you want them to remember you?

God bless, and get out there and be the best *you* possible.

ABOUT THE AUTHOR

Entrepreneur **CASSIDY PHILLIPS** made his mark with the revolutionary therapeutic company TriggerPoint. Combining his skills as an athlete, trainer, and biomechanical specialist with his passion for empowering others, Cassidy built TriggerPoint into a global brand that generated more than $60 million in sales while reaching over eighty countries.

Today, Cassidy puts his self-taught expertise to use as a consultant, venture capitalist, philanthropist, and speaker. He has dedicated his life to empowering those who are in need of a greater quality of life. He is an involved father and passionate husband and continues to live out his purpose-driven life.

Made in the USA
Columbia, SC
15 January 2019